D0206216

NEW LIGHT AND TRUTH

ROGER COLEMAN

NEW LIGHT AND TRUTH

THE MAKING OF
THE REVISED ENGLISH
BIBLE

OXFORD UNIVERSITY PRESS
CAMBRIDGE UNIVERSITY PRESS
1989

© Oxford University Press and Cambridge University Press 1989

First published 1989

Printed in Great Britain at the Bath Press, Avon

British Library cataloguing in publication data
Coleman, Roger
New light and truth.
1. Bible, English. Revised English
I. Title
220.5'2

ISBN 0 521 38497 4 (CUP) hard covers
ISBN 0 521 38171 1 (CUP) paperback
ISBN 0 19 101441 9 (OUP) hard covers

CONTENTS

v

PREFACE

This book offers a continuation of a story begun by the late Geoffrey Hunt: *About the New English Bible* (Oxford University Press and Cambridge University Press, 1970). In fact it has to cover some of the same ground, for the history of The New English Bible is the first part of the history of The Revised English Bible.

Like its predecessor, this little book does not set out to be an authoritative statement of the policies and aims of those who prepared the version of the Bible with which it is concerned; that is to be found in the Preface and the Introductions to the Old Testament, Apocrypha, and New Testament of The Revised English Bible itself. Its purpose is to provide some account of the background for those who are interested in knowing a little more about the version and the people who prepared it, as well as to record a factual outline of the work as a modest contribution to the history of Bible publishing.

The writer has been privileged to be entrusted by the University Presses with the editorial administration and coordination of the project throughout the major part of the revision, and also, from 1983 to 1989, to have acted as secretary to the supervising Joint Committee of the Churches. Any imperfections or errors within these pages are to be attributed solely to him, and not to the people more intimately concerned with the work to whom he is greatly indebted for advice and guidance.

CAMBRIDGE UNIVERSITY PRESS   R.C.
THE EDINBURGH BUILDING, CAMBRIDGE   *June 1989*

1. THE CLASSIC ENGLISH BIBLE

When I was a schoolboy it was commonly understood that the Bible in English was the Authorized Version of 1611 and no other. Such was the hold that the work of King James's translators had established over the mind and culture of the English-speaking world that reference to any other English version of Christian scripture needed careful preparation and explanation. When I competed for a school scripture reading prize in the months following the second world war, to have read 1 Corinthians 13 from the English Revised Version (despite its established use in higher education) would have been as unthinkable as reading from the Latin Vulgate. The Roman Catholic Douay–Reims Bible was not to be encountered in a protected Protestant environment; the Geneva Version – the popular English Protestant Bible which the AV superseded – was a bibliophile's prize whose identifying 'breeches' were no doubt a weird misprint in a text otherwise indistinguishable from the AV; the earlier Tudor versions lived only in the dusty footnotes of history books; the New Testament rendering in modern speech by R. F. Weymouth, like the American translation of Smith and Goodspeed, was as unknown as the American Standard Version; and James Moffatt's Bible was merely a curiosity produced by an eccentric Scotsman.

My schoolboy perceptions must have broadly reproduced those of the general public with no specialist knowledge of biblical matters. This was the lay background against which the General Assembly of the Church of Scotland in May 1946 debated a motion proposed by the Presbytery of Stirling and Dunblane 'that a translation of the Bible be made in the language of the present day'.

It was a revolutionary proposal. For years it had been tacitly assumed that any version of the scriptures in English laying claim to serious consideration, by Protestants at least, must take the AV as its point of departure. During the 1930s a proposal, likewise originating in Scotland, to bring up to date the Revised Version of 1881–5 had failed to find the necessary support to go ahead. In North America the revision of the American Standard Version (derived from the AV by way of the English Revised Version) had been authorized in 1937, and at the time of the Church of Scotland proposal the National Council of Churches of Christ was on the point of publishing the resulting New Testament – what was to become the Revised Standard Version of the Bible.

Two other recently published versions of the New Testament should also be remembered: that of The Bible in Basic English (1941), a rendering using a vocabulary of only 1000 words; and that of Monsignor Ronald Knox (1945), a translation from the Vulgate authorized for public use by the Roman Catholic Church. Despite its limited vocabulary, the Basic English Bible contrived to remain remarkably close in style and feeling to the AV; the Knox version, on the other hand, was unquestionably in modern English, if at times a little quaint or awkward.

It is easy to dismiss the preoccupation with the AV as the inevitable position of a conservative, middle-class religious establishment. But there was more to it than that. In the social flux brought about by the upheavals of the second world war, many Christians were beginning to have a bad conscience about sectarian barriers. The realization that a commonly used and universally loved Bible provided a living link between otherwise unreconciled Protestant denominations gave the AV a potential which went outside the normal role of scripture. In earlier years, new versions of the Bible (like that of J. N. Darby) had been associated with breakaway movements. The preservation of the AV had a contribution to make in the field of Christian unity.

At this time, too, there was growing interest in the new idea of 'the Bible as literature'. This was founded upon observation of the debt owed by English literary idiom to the King James Bible and its predecessors, but perhaps also motivated in some minds by the prospect of introducing religious revival through a secular, cultural back door.

But the strongest of all the forces contributing to the unassailability of the AV was a matter of pure superstition: the notion that the English of the early seventeenth century (or perhaps even earlier, for King James's men had adopted very largely the renderings and style of the Tudor versions) was the native language of the Holy Spirit. There is a tendency to think that religious authority and truth can only be communicated by means of a distinctive religious idiom: hence the skilful Jacobean pastiche of the mid-nineteenth-century Mormon scriptures. It was in deference to this view that the revisers of the AV in 1881 were instructed to retain the language of the Authorized or earlier versions rather than use the familiar vocabulary of their own day, and this was no doubt a factor in their failure to capture the attention and understanding of ordinary Bible readers.

That the Authorized Version answered the expectations of its mid-twentieth-century readers cannot be denied. Whether it conveyed its message to them effectively is another question altogether.

2. THE NEB STORY

It would be quite wrong to see the 1946 motion of the Presbytery of Stirling and Dunblane as an act of iconoclasm or cultural vandalism, though no doubt that was how it was viewed in some quarters at the time. In fact it grew out of a genuine need, experienced acutely and articulated repeatedly during and after the second world war by chaplains and other clergy, teachers, and youth workers, for a more accessible medium through which the Christian message could be delivered. The events and emotional atmosphere of wartime create a widespread search for religious experience, instruction, and understanding. The high proportion of members of the services from industrial urban backgrounds, unchurched and the products of an increasingly secular education, presented chaplains with a constituency for whom traditional scriptural language was virtually unintelligible. Likewise the civilian clergy found themselves at a disadvantage in dealing with displaced persons for whom any kind of English was a foreign tongue. The children encountered by teachers and youth workers came all too often from homes where first experience of religious concepts had been disrupted by the pressures of the times; religious education suffered from restrictions on school hours; evacuation or the absence of parents on war service took their toll of the conventional upbringing in which children of the middle classes at least would otherwise have an elementary understanding of religious ideas and language. A population to a large extent religiously illiterate was unlikely to bring immediate understanding to scripture in the idiom of three centuries or more earlier, however beautiful, solemn, or literary it might be.

The General Assembly received the proposal sympathetically, and made an approach to a number of other Churches, as a result of which a conference was convened at Westminster in the following October, when the delegates of the Church of Scotland were joined by Anglican, Methodist, Baptist, and Congregationalist representatives. The Bishop of Truro, the Right Reverend J. W. Hunkin, took the chair, and the Reverend Dr G. S. Hendry, who had initiated the original proposal from Stirling and Dunblane, was appointed secretary.

The conference unanimously agreed to recommend to the participating Churches that they should give their support to the preparation of a new translation avoiding all archaic words and forms of expression. The outline of their proposed translation policy is worth noting:

> That regard be paid to the native idiom and current usage of the English language; that Hebraisms, Grecisms and other un-English expressions be avoided; that freedom be employed in altering the construction of the original where that is considered necessary in order to make the meaning intelligible in English; and that the advice of one or more literary men [*sic!*] be sought regarding the quality of the translation.

Dr C. H. Dodd, Norris–Hulse Professor of Divinity in the University of Cambridge and one of the representatives of the Congregational Union, was commissioned to produce specimen translations of selected passages, and undertook to solicit the interest of the University Presses of Cambridge and Oxford.

A further conference was held in January 1947 with representatives of the two publishers in attendance, which resolved to ask the Churches represented to agree to the formal constitution of a 'Joint Committee on the New Translation of the Bible'. The new Committee duly met in Central Hall, Westminster, on 10 July 1947, and the chairman and secretary were confirmed in office, with Professor Dodd as vice-chairman.

The Committee made its first task the enlargement of the range of Churches represented: the Presbyterian Church of England and the Society of Friends (Quakers) entered into membership, and the Councils of Churches in Wales and Ireland were invited to appoint representatives; invitations were also issued to The British and Foreign Bible Society and The National Bible Society of Scotland. By late in 1947 the Committee had set up panels of scholars, seven in each case, to oversee the work on the Old and New Testaments, and agreement had been reached with the University Presses to finance and publish the translation in consideration of the copyright being vested in them jointly.

The methods and policy of the translators and literary advisers and the role of the Joint Committee have been described elsewhere* and need not detain us now. But it may be worth remembering the way in which the operational management of the translation evolved, since continuity in direction was to prove an important strength of the revision of the NEB in the years after 1970.

Professor Dodd's association with the project from its inception has already been noted. When it moved out of the experimental phase in 1949 and systematic translation began in earnest, an element of central control was seen to be essential, and Dodd was invited to become the overall coordinator with the title of General Director, while remaining convener of the New Testament translation panel. Another of the original representatives, Professor Theodore H. Robinson of the Baptist Union, was the first convener of the Old Testament panel, and subsequently also for a time assumed the convenership of the Apocrypha panel. Dr G. R. (later Sir Godfrey) Driver, Professor of Semitic Philology at Oxford, succeeded to the Old Testament convenership in 1957, and was named Deputy Director in 1961 after publication of The New English Bible New Testament. In the same

---

* Hunt, *About the New English Bible*, chapters II and III.

year the Apocrypha panel, whose work had fallen behind programme, was reconstituted, and Dr W. D. McHardy, Regius Professor of Hebrew at Oxford, who had been a member of the Old Testament panel from a very early stage, and had been nominated to strengthen the Apocrypha panel in 1958, was appointed convener for the Apocrypha. In 1965, with the complete translation almost ready for the publishers, Dodd and Driver were made Joint Directors, and in 1968 McHardy was named Deputy Director, acknowledging the special role he had played in acting for Driver as Old Testament convener during the latter's illness at a crucially late stage of the work.

In the same year the Archbishop of York, the Most Reverend Donald Coggan (subsequently Archbishop of Canterbury, and later Baron Coggan of Canterbury and Sissinghurst), became chairman of the Joint Committee of the Churches in succession to the late Bishop A. T. P. Williams, who had occupied the post since the death of Bishop Hunkin in 1950.

From the early days of the project it had been agreed that the translation would be published in two or more instalments, and the work on the New Testament had deliberately been allowed to run ahead of the remainder. When the Joint Committee gave its final approval to the text of the New Testament in March 1960 and agreed the publication date for a year later, the translation of the Old Testament and Apocrypha still had some way to go.

The publication of the NEB New Testament was an epoch-making event. The publishers had no real means of judging in advance what might be the public response to a translation of the Bible into contemporary language, but in the months before publication it began to be clear that this would by no means be a routine piece of publishing. It was acquiring the status of a national happening: a service in Westminster Abbey, a commemorative exhibition visited by the Queen, a

25-minute film on national television: this was promotional support of a different order from the conventional advertising and subscription activities to which the Presses were accustomed. As subscription to the trade proceeded, new reprints had to be commissioned in a continuing stream. Sales were being numbered in millions within weeks of publication.

As if there was not enough already to keep the new translation in the public eye, another event, unwelcome to the Joint Committee and the publishers alike, brought it on to the front pages of the newspapers. The holder of letters patent as the Queen's Printer, Messrs Eyre & Spottiswoode, claimed that the new translation fell within the scope of the 'privilege', or exclusive right granted by the sovereign to print Bibles and Prayer Books.

This grant, made to a succession of printers or publishers over the years, originated in the sixteenth century, and entitles the designated royal printer to protect his own business by restraining others in England and Wales from printing, publishing, or importing any Bibles or Prayer Books. For most of its history the privilege could only have referred in practical terms to the Authorized (King James) Version of the Bible and The Book of Common Prayer. The two University Presses, by virtue of a royal charter of 1534 authorizing Cambridge University to print 'all manner of books', and a parallel one granted to Oxford in 1628, are exempt from these restrictions. In 1881 the royal printer chose not to take part in publishing the Revised Version, the official revision of the AV, which was issued by the two University Presses alone. However, in June 1961 the Queen's Printer issued a challenge to the copyright in the new translation by publishing without permission a paperback of the Gospel according to John in the NEB text, asserting an equal right under the privilege to publish a translation of the Bible in the preparation of which he had made no investment.

From the point of view of the Presses, this was an infringement of the copyright which had been vested in them for a specific purpose by the Joint Committee of the Churches and, with the assent of the Joint Committee, they secured an injunction to prevent the Queen's Printer from distributing it, pending a hearing in the High Court. In 1963 Mr Justice Plowman decided in the Presses' favour that the NEB did not fall within the scope of the Bible privilege, and was subject to normal copyright at common aw.

In view of the wide enthusiasm and interest generated by the new translation it was not unexpected that there should be critical comment. In a report to the Joint Committee in the December after publication, Dodd noted that there had been 'several hundred criticisms and suggestions, which have come from various quarters, either in published reviews of the work, or in the seventy-odd letters that have been received', the majority reflecting nostalgia for the familiar phrases of the AV. The need for second thoughts about the New Testament text was recognized, but at the same time Dodd felt that actual changes should be minimal, to avoid changing the character of the translation, and only undertaken after time for reflection, so that the translators would not still be too much under the influence of the considerations that had produced the text as it stood. It was expected at this stage that the completion of the Old Testament and Apocrypha would take another four years, and it was agreed to defer the start of revising the New Testament until closer to that time, so that the revised New Testament could be first published as part of the complete Bible.

Accordingly a small revision committee began work in 1964, referring to the full New Testament panel and the Joint Committee for approval of changes, and a list of some 400 emendations, mostly of a very minor character, was finally approved in January 1966. The translation of the remainder of the Bible, however, was still not completed, the Apocrypha being submitted for the formal approval of the Joint Committee in July 1967, and the Old Testament in two stages in late 1968 and early 1969.

In the nature of things, the publication of the NEB complete with Old Testament and Apocrypha in March 1970 was unlikely to create as great a stir as the New Testament had done. In the first place, the English-speaking world had come to use and love the NEB New Testament, and to be familiar with its particular qualities. It had established itself, against the expectations of many, in the Churches; a book of Collects, Epistles and Gospels using the NEB text was published for the use of the Anglican Church in 1966. A number of editions differently bound and presented for a variety of purposes had come into use, some under the imprints of other publishers, including a paperback which was issued as the 2000th volume with the Penguin imprint. Audio recordings of the text had been made and sold widely. The eclectic Greek text underlying the translation had been published in 1964 by the University Presses as *The Greek New Testament* (ed. R. V. G. Tasker), and in the same year a concordance of words in the NEB New Testament differing from those of the AV was published by Marshall, Morgan & Scott. From 1963 onwards the volumes of the Cambridge Bible Commentary on the New English Bible began to be issued.

Not only was the NEB now a familiar object; it was no longer the unique version in contemporary English. In 1966 the New Testament in Today's English Version (later to become better known as the Good News Bible) was published in the USA. In the same year the Jerusalem Bible (a retranslation from the ancient languages of a text published in French with notes in 1956) first appeared in English. Made by Roman Catholic scholars, this was a complete version including those books which Roman Catholics regard as 'deuterocanonical' and are among those printed in the traditional Protestant Apocrypha.

Oddly, it was the publication of the NEB Apocrypha which

provided the greatest surprise for the publishers. The standard edition of the complete Bible was published in two forms, the Old and New Testaments with the Apocrypha and the two Testaments alone, having regard to those Christian Churches which do not accept the apocryphal books, or at any rate do not make significant use of them. Rather less than a third of the first printing was allocated to producing copies with the Apocrypha, but the shops soon reported that the two volumes were selling in more or less equal proportions. In many places the version with the Apocrypha was unobtainable by the end of publication day. After some months the relative demand for the Apocrypha began to ease, but it was clear that one of the earliest achievements of the complete NEB was to show that these secondary scriptures held much of value and interest to Christians which was not accessible in the difficult, at times impenetrable, text of King James's translators.

The publishing of the New Testament had provided the publishers with a good deal of information about the potential market for the complete Bible. However, because surprises, like the unexpected take-up of the Apocrypha, can always happen in publishing, they chose to take a cautiously flexible approach. Rather than print millions of copies at the outset, which could certainly have been justified by the demand and would have made impressive publicity if not good logistics, they chose to act circumspectly and step by step, printing and binding in a succession of smaller batches, but ensuring that adequate paper, materials, and production capacity were immediately available to meet a possibly fluctuating demand. In this way they were able to respond quickly to the unexpected popularity of the Apocrypha editions while avoiding the build-up of too large a stock, possibly of the wrong books, at any one time. All the same, the great demand caused frequent occasions during the first few months after publication when the publishers were unable to supply immediately, and it was not before August 1970 that the supply was able to cope with the demand in a steady way.

Two editions were available on publication, the standard edition with or without Apocrypha and a library edition in three volumes. The standard edition was published in cloth and a variety of leather bindings. At the time of publication a number of others were in preparation: an inexpensive New Testament, a lectern edition, and a pocket New Testament printed on india paper; all three made their appearance in 1971. At the end of 1970 a book of NEB *Readings for Holy Communion*, a one-year cycle with the alternatives and additions prescribed in the Anglican Series I services, appeared; in 1973 the Presses published a two-year cycle on similar lines based on the Series III services and with additional material for use in the Methodist Church. Negotiations were opened with other publishers about editions to be produced under licence for special markets: an illustrated and, later, a school, edition by The British and Foreign Bible Society, a Penguin paperback of the complete text, and an 'award' edition by Collins of Glasgow.

The successful marketing of any authoritative translation of the Bible demands the provision of ancillary study material. *A Companion to the New English Bible: New Testament* by A. E. Harvey had been commissioned in the early 1960s. In view of the changes in the text for the complete publication, the decision was made not to publish the companion until the October following the issue of the complete Bible. It subsequently appeared in a paperback edition, and the first part was reissued in paperback as a *Companion to the Gospels*. The last of the 17 New Testament volumes of the Cambridge Bible Commentary on the New English Bible had been published in 1967, and now the publishers were able to turn their attention to a further 37 books covering the Old Testament and Apocrypha, which appeared between 1972 and 1979. In order to provide a systematic account of the textual readings followed in the Old Testament, the Presses published in 1973 *The Hebrew Text of the Old Testament* by L. H. Brockington, which listed the readings adopted in the NEB which were at variance with those of Kittel's *Biblia Hebraica* (1937). In the USA there were further developments in the provision of study materials. The agreement covering the relationship between the American businesses of the two University Presses provided that they would collaborate in joint publishing of the NEB until the end of 1970, but that thereafter the two houses would be in competition and in a position to produce approved editions of the translation independently of one another. The American Branch of Cambridge University Press was first in the field in 1972 with an edition in traditional double-column Bible format incorporating a modest supplement in the form of an alphabetical Reader's Guide to biblical topics and names compiled by R. V. Glazebrook. In 1976 Oxford University Press Inc. produced a more elaborate 'Oxford Study Edition' under the general editorship of the biblical scholar Samuel Sandmel of the Hebrew Union College – Jewish Institute of Religion, Cincinnati, Ohio, with detailed annotations, introductory essays, and maps. Both these editions were later published jointly by Oxford and Cambridge outside the USA.

The establishment of the NEB as a widely accepted and authoritative standard text of the Bible in a literary style of some quality was evidenced in the many approaches made to the publishers for permission to quote or use it. The purposes of the many diverse applications ranged from quotation in works of scholarship, musical settings, and film and recording rights to a request to bind up the printed pages of the NEB in cases of genuine olive wood from the Holy Land. A number of translations were made directly from the NEB into foreign languages. An imaginative way of using the translation was found by The National Bible Society of Scotland when, jointly with the Edinburgh Medical Missionary Society, it proposed to publish an elegant reprint of Luke and Acts from the NEB under the title *A Physician's Story*, for presentation to medical graduands. Some of the approaches had to be resisted where the results might have been discreditable or in conflict with the policy of the Joint Committee and the publishers; in most cases they were warmly welcomed. In general it was the practice to grant free permission for use in any official prayer book or order of service of the Churches. Other applications were scrutinized carefully, and especially where any commercial exploitation was involved, an appropriate fee was charged as a contribution to the monumental cost of financing and publishing the translation, and of preparing its prospective revision.

3. WHY REVISE?

In his account of the making of The New English Bible, Geoffrey Hunt quotes a memorandum prepared by Professor Dodd towards the end of 1949, in which the Director outlined the 'Purpose and Intention of the Project'. Considering the novelty of the whole enterprise, it was a remarkably concise statement of the needs as they were perceived at the time, and of the principles which guided the translators in their work. 'How far it was carried out', Hunt adds, '. . . the readers of the NEB can now begin to judge.'

A generation later, we are entitled to extend the area of judgement, not so much with a view to allocating praise or blame, but to examine with the benefit of hindsight whether the priorities and emphases implied in Dodd's programme did accurately define some of the needs of the sixties and seventies and early eighties.

Dodd's memorandum begins with a statement that the new translation 'is not intended . . . for reading in church, nor is it directed, primarily, to those for whom the language of the AV and the Book of Common Prayer is the familiar and natural language of devotion'.

It seems strange that a statement so defensive and negative in tone should have sounded the keynote of the project, but the idea of the Bible being expressed in any language other than that of King James's men was for many out of the question. T. S. Eliot, invited in 1948 to act as a literary adviser to the project, excused himself on the grounds of prior commitments, but went on: 'Incidentally, however, I wonder whether there is any need for a new translation of the Bible, and also whether any contemporary English is likely to be good enough for the purpose. I should have thought that a text of the authorised version provided with notes of correc-

Lord Coggan, Chairman of the Joint Committee, and Roger Coleman,
Secretary, and Co-ordinating Editor for the two University Presses

tion where the Jacobean translators have gone wrong is all that is really needed.' His view was echoed by others. In such a climate of opinion, to suggest that a translation in contemporary language might be used for reading aloud in the worship of the Churches – much of which was derived indirectly if not borrowed verbatim from the AV – was quite unacceptable. It was acknowledged that the translators of 1611 had made mistakes, and that the revisers of 1881 had not always attained their predecessors' literary elegance, but the abandonment of the traditional formulas and familiar phrases in church was not seen as a practical possibility.

Hence the insistence by Dodd and the other leaders of the project that there should be no thought of superseding the AV in worship. But by the time the NEB was published in its entirety another movement was well under way to challenge the universal use of the 1611 version for liturgical purposes. In 1965 the Church of England secured the adoption of the Alternative Services Measure, by which Parliament sanctioned the experimental use of new forms of service, designed to serve more appropriately the needs of a Church adapting itself to the thought, speech, and practice of the mid-twentieth century. The first series of alternative services published under the authority of the Measure corresponded closely to the forms of the 1928 Prayer Book, which had been rejected by Parliament but had nevertheless been widely used within the Church. The language of the 1928 Prayer Book and the first alternative services showed no real movement away from the familiar phrases looking back to Cranmer and the AV, and the printed-out biblical readings were all taken from the Revised Version. But a second series of alternative services, and especially the third series which were approved by the Anglican General Synod from 1970 onwards, deliberately moved on from the traditional language. So far, in fact, that when the results of the experimentation came to be more permanently adopted in *The Alternative Service Book 1980* the compilers were careful to step back from innovations ('Do not put us to the test' in the Lord's Prayer, for example) that had affronted some Anglican worshippers. *The Alternative Service Book* printed out biblical readings from several twentieth-century English versions of the Bible, some 30 per cent of which were from the NEB, but it is significant that none of these included passages embodying prayer, with their retention of the 'thou' form of address to God.

At the same time other Churches were also ceasing to rely on traditional language in their services. The abandonment by the Roman Catholic Church of the Latin Mass in favour of the use of vernacular language, following the Second Vatican Council in 1963, was perhaps the most radical of the changes made across the whole spectrum of the Christian Churches.

Whatever may have been the perceptions of 1946–50, by the time the complete NEB was published in 1970, a version of the Bible still using thou-language, if only in part, and presented as something to be used alongside and in explanation of the AV, was already in some sense out of date. It was a testimony to the excellence of the NEB in all other respects that it became so widely accepted and used.

The three elements of the 'public in view', as defined by Dodd in the 1949 memorandum, were by implication a middle-class constituency. Although there was a limited evangelistic intention directed towards the unchurched, the language that would have suggested a programme aimed at a broad social and educational range is, perhaps significantly, absent. An appeal to the less well educated, or to those whose first language was not English, was not part of the programme.

The first target public was not only middle class; it was also a secular readership: 'the large section of the population which has no effective contact with the Church ... sufficiently educated to understand quite a lot of the Bible, if it were put before them in language which was acceptable'. If Dodd's claim that such people were often 'keenly interested to know what the Bible is about' was valid, it should perhaps have been questioned whether, in the second half of the twentieth century, that interest would be ideally satisfied by providing something planned as the explication of a seventeenth-century text. There was more than a hint here of acceptance that the language used in the Churches would remain immutably archaic, and to bring people back into the circle of worshippers it would be necessary to familiarize them with Jacobean religious diction. Within two decades there was ample evidence that such an assumption was wholly mistaken.

Dodd's second target public was children 'being educated in "modern" schools of various kinds, for whom the Bible . . . must be made "contemporary"'. Expressing the hope that the AV would continue to be the medium of instruction, he proposed that a second version should be provided as a key to the meaning. Reference was evidently being made to the Bible as a medium of *religious* instruction, for this document dates from a time before the muting of specifically Christian in favour of pluralistic religious education, and before the emergence at school level of the serious possibility of studying the Bible as literature. Just as preferences in the language of worship shifted from an archaic to a contemporary idiom, so educational preferences (whatever the object of teaching which involved the use of the Bible) shifted in the direction of exclusively using a contemporary version.

The third public was effectively a churchgoing readership for whom the familiar AV text had gone stale and lost its impact. It seems odd that in this of all contexts the leaders of the NEB project should have been content that the new version should be limited to serving as an adjunct to, and not a substitute for, something that had (in their view) become ineffective.

The aim of the translation was sound enough, even though it fell short of what it might have attained. The problem, not fully perceived by the Joint Committee or the translators in 1949, was that the aim was directed towards a moving target. Some sense of this does, it is true, emerge from their later deliberations. For example, it was questioned at a meeting of the Joint Committee with the members of the translation panels in 1957 whether the policy of using 'thou' for address to God in prayer ought to be reconsidered, and for a time it seemed possible that the result would be a mixture of 'thou' and 'you' readings. The proposal surfaced again in 1966, in view of the increasing use of the plural pronoun in liturgical worship, but it was recognized that this would entail such radical changes at a late stage of the translation work that there would inevitably be unacceptable delays in the publication of the complete NEB. After publication the problem became even more acute, when in 1973 the Anglican Church Information Office published with permission a number of NEB lections in an experimental set of *Lessons for Holy Communion Series III*, in which, for good liturgical reasons but without authorization, textual changes were made, including 'thou' to 'you'. When the University Presses' own book of *Readings for Holy Communion* appeared later in the year, 'thou' was restored, though other modifications were accepted, notably to the openings of the lections so as to make full sense of a passage removed from its context.

The 'thou' problem was clearly in the minds of the Joint Committee when they began considering in 1969 what ongoing provision should be made for their role as governing body after publication of the complete NEB. The idea of a revision of the Old Testament and Apocrypha in the not too distant future was accepted without question, if only to extend to them the benefit of the kind of second thoughts which the New Testament had received in 1964–6, but the eventual resolution to reconstitute the Joint Committee after publication seemed to contemplate a revised edition of the whole translation in about ten years' time.

For the same reasons that had prompted Dodd to recommend delaying the first revision of the New Testament until the amended version could be published with the Old Testament and Apocrypha, no immediate action was taken about commissioning a revision. The new Committee (now formally renamed The Joint Committee on The New English Bible) first met in December 1971, and the appointment of Professor McHardy as third Joint Director was agreed with acclamation. Dodd reported that critical comments on the new text were still coming in, though the stream was diminishing; it was the last report he was to make on the translation over which he had presided with such skill and care and dedication, for he died at the age of 89 three months before the Joint Committee's next meeting at the end of 1973.

4. THE GOVERNING BODY

The Joint Committee on The New English Bible may have looked very like the body which had come into being in 1947 to plan and direct the new translation which was to become the NEB. But it was significantly different in a number of ways.

Foremost in importance was a change in the status of two of its members, those representing the Roman Catholic Church in England and Wales and in Scotland. Following an expression of interest in the translation by members of the two hierarchies, the Joint Committee had in 1966 invited their participation in the work. From July of that year, Roman Catholic representatives had attended meetings with the status of observer. At the last meeting of the old Committee the possibility of public use of the NEB in Roman Catholic worship had been discussed, and it was reported that three minor changes would pave the way to the Church's recognition of the NEB as an accepted version. Since these changes involved no alteration to the text of the translation, but simply the transposition of one verse (the 'short ending' of Mark) and two emendations to the introductory matter, the Joint Committee readily agreed to their being made. They expressed the hope that Roman Catholic representatives would be present as fully participating members, and it was with this status that they attended the first meeting of the new Committee. At this meeting the Joint Committee resolved to renew an invitation to the Irish hierarchy of the Roman Catholic Church to take part. The invitation was duly accepted, and the Roman Catholics of Ireland were represented from the following meeting onwards.

The Joint Committee in the Jerusalem Chamber, Westminster Abbey, in June 1978

Of those who attended the initial meetings of the Church representatives in 1946 and 1947 only two remained, the Congregationalist member the Revd John Huxtable and Professor Dodd himself, another member of the Congregational Church. The original membership had since been enlarged by the addition of the Presbyterian Church of England, the Religious Society of Friends, and the representatives of the Churches in Ireland and Wales nominated by the Councils of Churches for those two countries.

In function, too, the new Committee was different. It began with no programme of action; the brief it gave itself was a watching one, 'to take oversight of The New English Bible during the next years, and eventually be responsible for the new edition expected in about ten years'.

The Committee was conscious that, although it represented numerically a very large proportion of Christian church members in the British Isles, there might be other Churches with members who were already NEB readers which would be prepared and perhaps eager to collaborate in the work. A small subcommittee was set up to investigate where support might be found, and as a result invitations to send representatives were accepted by the Moravian Church in Great Britain and Ireland and by the Salvation Army.

As well as 'substantive' representatives, most Churches have nominated 'alternate' members who have deputized for the substantive members when they have been unable to attend meetings, and have provided a valuable reserve of informed support for the Committee's work.

The British and Foreign Bible Society (now known as the Bible Society) and The National Bible Society of Scotland, which had been invited by the Churches to send representatives to the meetings of the Joint Committee from the early days of their work on the NEB, have also continued to take part. The University Presses have each normally been represented at meetings of the Joint Committee by their most senior editorial executive and the senior executive responsible specifically for Bible publishing.

Thanks to the Dean and Chapter of Westminster, home to the Joint Committee of the Churches has been the Jerusalem Chamber in the Abbey – as it had been to the London company of translators who produced the Authorized Version of 1611 and to its Revisers of 1881–5. The meetings have normally taken place at the beginning of each December, although early in the revision period the Committee met only in alternate years, and in the later stages two meetings a year were sometimes necessary. An Executive Committee, consisting of the Chairman, Directors, Secretary, and representatives of the Presses, has prepared the work of the full Committee, and on occasion taken interim decisions on its behalf or (in relation to preparing the Preface and Introductions to the REB) acted as an editorial committee.

A complete list of those who participated in the work of the Joint Committee may be found in Appendixes II and III below.

The period of the watching brief soon came to an end, and the Joint Committee began to give active guidance to the Director of Revision on revision policy and method, and to approve the appointment of revisers. The involvement of members in examining and making critical comments on the draft revision (see pages 39–40) was an important ingredient in the successful completion of the work.

The approach of the new version brought into focus an issue of some delicacy: what its name should be. The radical nature of the revision needed to be reflected in the title, and yet the NEB's strengths would all, it was hoped, be present and probably enhanced in the new version. It would be necessary to show continuity in order to retain the interest of those who had adopted the NEB, but at the same time desirable to indicate that here was something for those who were seeking an altogether new translation. A great many suggestions were made, and the advice of the Presses was sought.

Since it was apparent that the wide adoption of the NEB in churches and in schools was not something that could be set aside overnight, it seemed wise to maintain the NEB in print after the new version was published, and in that case 'New English Bible Second (*or* Revised) Edition' would simply confuse. Eventually, after a debate that spanned two years, 'The Revised English Bible' was chosen, and the Joint Committee was known from December 1987 onwards as The Joint Committee on the Revised English Bible. General assent was given to the proposal that the NEB should be maintained in print, at least for some time after publication of its successor. To place the REB on the same copyright footing as the NEB, the Joint Committee agreed in 1987 to assign to the University Presses of Oxford and Cambridge the copyright in the changes that it had adopted on the recommendation of the revisers.

Members of the Joint Committee, mindful of their responsibilities to their parent Churches, took considerable interest in the way the REB would be presented and promoted to its potential readers, and often found irksome the confidentiality that it was necessary to preserve until the new Bible came close to realization, especially in so far as church education programmes, for example, were being planned for the years ahead without knowledge of this new rendering of the scriptures. Matters of revision strategy, like the developments leading to the appointment of the New Testament reviewing subcommittee (see page 41) or the philosophy of textual subheadings, excited lively discussion, while at the same time the members were ready to devote intense interest to questions of detail like the rendering of *doxa* or *en Christo*. Early in 1988 the members of the Joint Committee were able to confirm formally to the Churches they represented that the work of the revision had been completed, and thus render account of a patient and enthusiastic stewardship.

Their work did not end there, however, and many members took an active part in making the new version known within the Churches they represented, guiding the Presses in promotional activities and presiding or speaking at presentations to denominational groups and conferences. At a last meeting in June 1989, they resolved to bring the existence of the Joint Committee formally to an end on publication of the REB in September 1989, but to recommend to the publishers the establishment of an ongoing committee of four representatives of the Churches. This group – three members of the existing Joint Committee and one of the revisers who worked on the REB – would watch over the future success of the revised translation, provide advice to the Presses, and have the power to reconvene a conference of all the participating Churches when the need arose in the future.

5. ORGANIZING THE REVISION

The moment of decision for the new Joint Committee arrived in December 1973. A survey of the comments and criticisms received had been made earlier in the year. The advanced years of Professor Dodd and the failing health of Sir Godfrey Driver had made it virtually impossible that either of them should play more than an advisory part in any revision, and it was clear that the main responsibility would fall on the shoulders of Professor McHardy. The fact that most attention – apart from the 'thou' problem – would need to be paid to the Old Testament and Apocrypha, in the translation of which he had played a leading role from the earliest stages, made McHardy the best possible choice; the Joint Committee duly appointed him 'Director in charge of revision' and commissioned him to begin the work.

In December 1973 the task of producing a revision of the NEB for prospective publication in 1980 did not seem a particularly daunting one. Since two years would be needed for printing and publication, four clear years could be devoted to the textual revision itself. It would be some months before any work could start, and the Joint Committee arranged to meet again in June 1974 to approve nominations of scholars to the revising committees. These committees, they resolved, should be small, perhaps with no more than three members plus the Director of Revision acting as convener. At this stage 'literary' attention to the text was still seen as a separate and systematic operation, and the literary experts were referred to informally and quaintly as 'Englishers', as distinct from the translational 'revisers'. But there was consciousness of the stultifying effect of a large literary committee, evidenced by a proviso that a single individual might be appointed to take care of the literary aspects of the entire version. It was also

Professor W.D. McHardy, Director of Revision

thought that some books of the NEB might require no revision except from a literary point of view.

Nevertheless, when McHardy returned to the Joint Committee the following June with his first list of nominees, the literary section contained as many as four names, with the promise of others to be nominated 'as the need arises'. But he was careful to add that they were to provide help on a flexible basis and not to be regarded as a committee.

At this planning stage, before the Director and his revisers had had experience in practice of what the work might entail, two revising committees only were proposed, one for the Old Testament, and one for the New Testament which, with additional help, would also be responsible for the Apocrypha. This more or less reflected the Joint Committee's outline assessment of the nature of the revision in 1973:

> It was clear that the O.T. needed a thorough revision. The Apocrypha seemed to require something less thorough, but it needed polishing, and some new material would have to be used in revision. Certain consequent changes would have to be made in the N.T., as well as some modification in the light of the use already made of it.

The first revision meeting, a New Testament session at Professor McHardy's rooms in the Oriental Institute at Oxford on 27–30 September 1974, was approached in an atmosphere of excited anticipation, though its minutes are limited to the laconic record: 'The Committee revised Mark 1 to 8:26.' Present with the Director and his secretary Isobel Garrard were Dr Morna Hooker (University Lecturer in New Testament at Oxford; later Lady Margaret's Professor of Divinity at Cambridge), Dr George Caird (Principal of Mansfield College, Oxford, and Reader in Biblical Studies; later Dean Ireland's Professor of Biblical Exegesis), and Canon Maurice Wiles (Regius Professor of Divinity at Oxford). The Director, who had been asked by the Joint Committee to pursue the NEB policy of ignoring denominational affiliations and to empanel revisers solely on the strength of their scholarship, took an almost perverse pleasure in looking round the table at a Methodist, a Congregationalist, and an Anglican.

The inaugural Old Testament session followed hard on its heels on 1–4 October at Ely House, the elegant eighteenth-century office of Oxford University Press in London. Here, with a slight change in the ecumenical formula, were a Methodist, a Roman Catholic, and an Anglican: Dr George Anderson (Professor of Hebrew and Old Testament Studies at Edinburgh), Father Robert Murray, S J (Lecturer at Heythrop College, London), and Dr Ernest Nicholson (Dean of Pembroke College, Cambridge, and University Lecturer in Divinity; later Oriel Professor of Divinity at Oxford). In their first four days the team managed to work through the first 37 chapters of Genesis.

Initially different approaches were adopted for the two Testaments. The New Testament team, with less material to consider, began by going through the entire text of Mark verse by verse. On the other hand the Old Testament revisers, conscious of the pressure of the programme on their much longer text, proposed at this stage to deal only with specific points raised by members of the team, as well as the adjustment of thou-language and points which had been filed for attention as a result of reviews and written comments received. The Director of Revision had written to solicit suggestions about points for consideration from some of the original translators and others with a special interest in the NEB. Until a stable pattern of working emerged, it was decided not to devote too much time to points of major difficulty, but to cover as much ground as possible and return to the most serious problems later. The decision to reduce if possible the number of footnotes was made at an early stage. This reflected the intention initially to publish in one edition only; the two editions of the NEB in 1970 had made it possible to print two levels of annotation, with the library edition including all the notes, and the standard edition omitting two categories thought to be outside the concerns of the more general reader.

These early meetings, though they accomplished much in the way of actual revision, were essentially of importance as a means of exploring the territory to be covered and of developing and testing the methods which were to be employed. By the end of 1974 the New Testament group had spent 51 hours in full session and had dealt with about half of Matthew and the whole of Mark. The Old Testament group had in a total of 66 hours covered most of Genesis, all of Exodus and Leviticus, and a substantial part of Numbers.

In addition to the plenary sessions in which the revision teams resolved problems in discussion, each member spent much time individually in preparation and research into the points at issue by studying commentaries and the specialized scholarly literature.

It was not until January 1975 that the Apocrypha team first convened, the anticipated task before it being less extensive than that of the others. This was a smaller group in which the Director was joined by Dr Sebastian Brock, Lecturer in Aramaic and Syriac at Oxford, and Dr Colin Roberts, a classical scholar and former Secretary to the Delegates of Oxford University Press, who had represented the Press at meetings of the Joint Committee from 1954 onwards.

As 1975 progressed, more revisers were drawn into the Old and New Testament teams. The Joint Committee did not meet again until late in 1976, when the names of practically all the additional revisers were submitted and warmly approved. A complete list of those involved appears in Appendix IV on page 81.

In order to secure the best possible combination of knowledge, skill, and personality to work on different texts with their own special kinds of problem, the Director felt himself at liberty to change the composition of the teams book by book, only observing the rule that in each case at least one member of the group apart from himself should be familiar with the method of working from having participated in earlier sessions on another book. The presence of revisers with substantial earlier experience also helped to maintain consistency in the character and extent of the changes made. In the earlier stages of the work, before the full range of what was needed had been grasped by the policy makers, it is true that the revisers had tended to be very restrained in their proposals. But later, as the scope was seen to be enlarged, there was sometimes an urge to make all things new, and it was necessary to recall firmly that the enterprise was, after all, a revision.

Serious divisions among the revisers were rare, and never along denominational lines. A guiding principle adopted by the Director in cases of disagreement, recalled with appreciation by the revisers, was 'Let the text have a vote,' i.e. 'Give greatest weight to what the NEB says.'

A flexible approach was also adopted to the involvement of the 'literary men', a goodly proportion of whom turned out to be women. In retrospect it had seemed to the representatives of the Churches that the committee approach to monitoring English style had been one of the least satisfactory aspects of the making of the NEB, and in the revision there was no committee discussion or decision-making of a literary character, except when the literary comments were referred back to the revision panels themselves. Members of the Joint Committee pointed out, in the course of a significant discussion of the use of literary panels, that the translational revisers themselves were – or ought to be – skilled in the use of English, and the formal, committee approach to 'Englishing' should be redundant and could be counter-productive. The stage at which the script was first submitted to literary scrutiny varied. Where there was concern about the overall presentation of a particular book in the NEB, and there seemed to be a need for prior stylistic advice for the revisers, the unrevised text would be shown individually to one or more advisers, and their comments would be fed back to the revisers as they proceeded with their work. In other cases the basic revision would be carried out before the script was offered for comment on style. The choice would typically depend on how much translational alteration seemed to be needed. As the editorial staffs of the Presses became involved in the processing of the scripts, the Director also encouraged them to comment on matters of style and presentation.

The target publication date of 1980 implied that the completely revised text would be ready for the printer early in 1978. The work in accordance with the originally very limited aims had indeed been more or less completed by this time, although it had not yet been shown to the Joint Committee or received any kind of attention from the publishers. But close and critical attention to the translation by the revision teams had brought to light many points than meant going back over ground already covered, some of which are discussed in chapter 6 below. The implications of abandoning thou-language were now seen to be far wider than expected, for the adjustments made to passages containing the singular pronoun tended to make them inconsistent in style with others in which surviving 'biblicisms' (see page 44 below) had hitherto seemed tolerable. The problem of 'briticisms' – words used and understood differently in Britain from other English-speaking countries – was one of the subjects on the agenda of a visit by the Director to North America for consultations with scholars and others during the summer of 1978. The question of gender-inclusive language had not been addressed in a serious, let alone systematic, way before the end of the 1970s. The completion in 1977 of a new edition of Kittel's *Biblia Hebraica*, which had formed the textual basis for the NEB Old Testament translation but was now some 40 years old, suggested re-examination of some passages. The 26th edition (1979) of *Novum Testamentum Graece*, edited by Aland and others, prompted reconsideration of some aspects of the eclectic text on which the NEB New Testament had been based. By 1977, 1980 was no longer seen as a realistic publication date, though 1981 was still being mentioned, with hope rather than assurance; by 1981, hopes centred on spring 1985.

In the summer of 1982 Professor McHardy left Oxford, where the revision work had been organized from the offices of the University Press, to return to his home town of Cullen in Scotland. The move, and the transfer of archives and working papers not immediately needed to the offices of Cambridge University Press, were accomplished with surprisingly little disruption to the revision programme. Indeed, since the revision work at the time was concentrated on teams based in Scotland, their meetings were in some ways made easier. The Director's move, and the stage which the work had now reached, made it important to develop a new mode of operation to take account of three factors: first, that there was no immediate access by the Director and his teams to the comprehensive administrative services including typing and copying which they had enjoyed in Oxford; second, that the stage was being approached at which it would be vital to involve the members of the Joint Committee of the Churches directly in the assessment and approval of the new version; third, that pressure for speedy completion of the remaining stages of the work was now becoming intense.

At its meeting in December 1983 on the tenth anniversary of the commissioning of the revision, the Joint Committee was presented with a booklet reproducing a selection of extended passages in their current revised state. A long and lively discussion took place, ranging over many aspects of the style and presentation. It was clear that the Committee would not be content to be a mere rubber stamp for the revisers' work. A member had defined its role at an earlier meeting thus: 'The Committee represents the concern of the Churches for the nature of the translation; provides recognition of its quality; is in a position to commend it to the Churches; and gives advice and guidance to the Presses.' This was not a job description to be taken lightly.

The need to make the texts of the revised books available for the Committee's scrutiny and comment helped to determine the Presses' own investigation into the best means of composition for printing which would allow of adjustments being made up to a very late stage, while keeping the high cost of reading and proof correction to a minimum (see chapter 7 below). In the spring of 1984 the Director began releasing to the Presses typescript texts of the books, on the effective completion of the revision work. These were keyboarded on to word-processor disks, proofread (including a systematic reading aloud), and printed out in typescript to be ready for submission to the Joint Committee.

In his description of the procedure adopted in the making of the NEB, Geoffrey Hunt mentions what were known as 'pink books', containing the translation panels' final drafts, which were circulated to every member of the Joint Committee for information and consideration. The same procedure was at first contemplated for the revision, but was not adopted. Unlike the NEB, the REB was not something absolutely new, but a revision of an approved translation that already existed. Many of the Joint Committee were very busy people and could not expect to examine conscientiously every word; they might even be discouraged, by the sheer weight of material, from looking at books on which they would have a special contribution to offer because of their own expertise or interest, or because of doctrinal sensitivities of the Church they represented. So it was decided to give members the opportunity to select for examination those books which would be of particular interest or importance to them. It happened that in this way every book received serious scrutiny by one or more members of the Joint Committee, and a very substantial number of constructive criticisms, suggestions, and comments were sent in to the Presses for consideration by the Director and his team. As they were received the comments were accumulated in chapter and verse order on the word processor, so that they could be worked through in order and multiple comments on the same passage could be considered simultaneously.

As the examination of the texts on this selective basis went forward, concern began to be voiced about whether this provided a sufficiently full and systematic review of the New Testament, the most sensitive area from a doctrinal point of view, to enable the Joint Committee to commend the revision without reservation to the Churches. There was every confidence in the revisers, but there would have been no overall appraisal by a third party standing at a distance from their actual work. The concern was reinforced by two other considerations: the knowledge that some variations had been adopted from the readings published in Tasker's edition of the Greek text referred to on page 11; and the death in the spring of 1984 of Professor Caird, a key figure among the New Testament revisers because of his comprehensive linguistic skills. (The story is told that early in his career Caird was appointed to a professorship in a Canadian university, partly on the strength of a very high recommendation from England. Just before he took up the post the university realized in some embarrassment that it had offered an Old Testament chair to someone whose doctoral research had been in the New Testament. They cabled the referee, 'Can Caird teach Hebrew?' 'Yes,' was the reply, 'and if you give him an hour's notice he can also teach Aramaic, Syriac, Coptic, Akkadian, Soghdian and Sumerian.') Caird's death came a few days after the completion of the revision work of the committees in which he had participated, but his absence would be particularly keenly felt when the revisers came to consider the questions raised about the translation by Joint Committee members.

The need for an independent review was debated at some length by the Joint Committee. It was unacceptable that such a review should be conducted by people, however authoritative, who were not fully imbued with the principles, policies, and methods which the representatives of the Churches themselves had approved. Accordingly they welcomed a proposal by the Chairman to set up a reviewing subcommittee of appropriately qualified members of the Joint Committee itself to conduct a comprehensive review of the New Testament text on its behalf, to make recommendations to the revisers where this was thought necessary, and to consider jointly with them any divergence of views about the text or its translation. This was a task which could not be accomplished without the investment of a great deal of time and work by those involved – including the revisers, who by this time had assumed that their own work was virtually over. The Committee invited Professor Grayston and Canon Harvey, both distinguished New Testament scholars who had published authoritative books based on the NEB, to act as the reviewing subcommittee, and they began their work in the second half of 1985, each carrying out on his own a systematic word by word examination of the entire version, taking into account also the suggestions and comments of the rest of the Joint Committee. Together they then prepared extensive lists of jointly agreed criticisms and comments for the consideration of the revision teams. Each team of revisers studied the reviewers' comments, either adopting them or providing explanation of their reasons for not doing so. After the reviewing subcommittee had examined these responses, the two groups then met together to settle outstanding divergences of view. It was not until the late summer of 1987 that the final meetings between the reviewers and the two revision teams had taken place, and the reviewers reported to the Joint Committee at its December meeting that all questions had been resolved in general agreement.

Simultaneously with the work of the reviewing subcommittee, attention was being given to a review of the textual subheadings throughout the Bible (see pages 54–55 below). Work had also been proceeding on the Joint Committee's comments on the Apocrypha and Old Testament. Spread over a year or so, the finally amended texts were sent in batches to the Presses for copy editing. By the time the last of the confirmed copy was ready for the copy editor in November 1988 the revision process had been in train for fourteen years and two months.

6. THE NEW VERSION

The revision of a Bible in modern English was if anything a more novel procedure than making a contemporary translation in the first place. The Joint Committee of the Churches had given the revisers two broad tasks: substituting 'you' for 'thou', and reviewing criticisms received. There were no means by which they could have foreseen the range of further adjustments that these two operations might make necessary, no way in which they could have formulated an exhaustive set of positive instructions or even specified where the limits of the revisers' tasks might lie. It was the job of the revisers, and more specifically that of the Director, to develop a definition as they went along.

So it was that the scope and character of the revision grew and changed shape as the revisers pursued their work. The need for this is most easily seen in the context of amending 'theee' and 'thou'. Once the pronouns and associated verb forms were changed it often happened that other phrases in the same context suddenly appeared old-fashioned or over-literary. For example, when some such phrase as 'the words which thou hast uttered' became 'the words which you have uttered', the revisers would immediately notice that 'uttered' was a misfit, even though it read perfectly well with thou-language. Returning to the text, the revisers might find that 'the words which you have spoken' read more naturally. But then they may have looked again and seen that the relative pronoun and the compound past tense would not be used in this context in late twentieth-century speech; once again reviewed, the phrase might eventually be rendered 'the words you spoke' without any loss in style or meaning, and with a gain in force and clarity. Such changes could not be adopted by rule of thumb; it was necessary in each case to balance the amended phrase against the surrounding passage and adjust either the emendation or perhaps the context accordingly.

Apart from the use of 'thou' in the language of prayer, the NEB's claim to be in the language of the present day was not seriously contested. Yet there was one feature of the translation which could not always stand up to rigorous examination in this respect. The language used by Christians in a religious context is in great part derived from the Bible. Because its phrases have continued in active use in the Churches over a long period, the Bible to which they refer is usually a traditional one, and in many cases their vocabulary and style reproduce those of the AV. In practical terms we may still choose to regard this as contemporary language, because it is part and parcel of current religious discourse and of the (in some cases self-consciously) contemporary liturgy of the Churches. It can be seen, for example, in the hybrid language of the Collects of the Anglican *Alternative Service Book 1980*, in survivals such as 'beseech', 'ever' (= always), 'evermore', 'save' (= except), 'that' (= so that), and so on. But this is not the written or spoken language of the present day as it is commonly used, and to some people it may suggest that religious language has a tendency to become a thing apart, an esoteric form of communication for initiates.

Many such locutions from 'church' language were, probably unwittingly, written into the NEB. Expressions which owe their continuing use to liturgical language borrowed from the AV came to be referred to as 'biblicisms' during the course of the revision. The revisers did not try to exclude such features altogether, for that would have impoverished the stylistic range of the translation. But, for example, the 'biblical' reversal of the first and third person auxiliaries 'shall' and 'will' in plain future tenses was often amended; 'O' as a word of address was generally abandoned; 'in the day' was changed to 'on the day' when modern usage preferred it; and a number of similar out-of-date words and phrases were likewise adjusted.

3 through the camp, ~~[and gave this order to the people]~~ 'When you see the Ark of the Covenant of the LORD your God being carried forward by the levitical priests, then you too ~~[shall]~~ leave your positions 4 and set out. Follow it, but do not go close to it; keep some distance behind, about ~~[a]~~ thousand ~~[yards]~~. ~~This~~ will show you the ~~way~~ you are to ~~[go]~~, for you have not travelled 5 this way before.' Joshua ~~then~~ said to the people, '~~[Hallow]~~ yourselves, for tomorrow the LORD will ~~[do]~~ a 6 great miracle among you.' To the priests he said, 'Lift ~~[up]~~ the Ark of the Covenant and ~~[pass in front]~~ of the people.' So they lifted ~~[up]~~ ~~the Ark of the Covenant~~ and went ~~in~~ 7 ~~[front]~~ of the people. [Then the LORD said to Joshua, 'Today I ~~[will]~~ begin to ~~[make]~~ you ~~[stand high]~~ in the eyes of all Israel, and they ~~[shall]~~ know that I ~~[will]~~ be with you as I was with 8 Moses. Give ~~[orders]~~ to the priests who carry the Ark of the Covenant ~~[and tell them that when they]~~ come to the edge of the waters of the Jordan, ~~[they]~~ are to take ~~[their]~~ stand in the river.' 9 ~~[Then]~~ Joshua said to the Israelites, '~~[Come here]~~ and listen to the 10 words of the LORD your God. ~~[By]~~ this you ~~[shall]~~ know that the living God is among you and that he will drive out before you the Canaanites, ~~[the]~~ Hittites, ~~[the]~~ Hivites, ~~[the]~~ Perizzites, ~~[the]~~ Girgashites, ~~[the]~~ 11 Amorites, and ~~[the]~~ Jebusites[the Ark of the Covenant of ~~[the LORD]~~, the ~~[lord]~~ of all the earth[is to cross 12 the Jordan at your head. Choose[twelve men from the tribes of Israel, one ~~[man]~~ from each tribe. 13 ~~[When]~~ the priests carrying the Ark of the LORD, the ~~[lord]~~ of all the earth, set foot in the waters of the Jordan, then the waters of the Jordan will be cut off; the water coming down from upstream will stand 14 piled up like a bank.' ~~[So the]~~ people set out from their ~~[tents]~~ to cross the Jordan, with the priests in front ~~of~~

~~[then]~~ carrying the Ark of the Covenant. Now the Jordan is in full 15 flood in all its reaches throughout the time of harvest[~~When~~ the priests reached the Jordan and ~~[dipped]~~ their feet ~~[in]~~ the water at 16 the edge, the water ~~[coming]~~ down from upstream was brought to a standstill; it piled up like a bank for a long way back, as far as Adam, a town near Zarethan, The water[coming down to the ~~[Sea]~~ of the Arabah, the Dead Sea, ~~[were]~~ completely cut off, and the people crossed over opposite Jericho. The 17 priests carrying the Ark of the Covenant of the LORD stood ~~[firm]~~ on the dry bed in the middle of the ~~[Jordan]~~; and all Israel passed over on dry ground[until the whole nation had ~~[crossed the river]~~

WHEN the whole nation had ~~[finished crossing]~~ the Jordan, the LORD 4 said to Joshua, '~~[Take]~~ twelve men 2 from the people, one from each tribe, and order them to ~~[lift]~~ up 3 twelve stones from this place, ~~[out of]~~ the middle of the Jordan, where the ~~[feet of the]~~ priests ~~[stood firm]~~ They are to carry ~~[them]~~ across and ~~[set]~~ them ~~[down]~~ in the camp where 4 you spend the night.' Joshua summoned the twelve ~~[men]~~ whom he had ~~[chosen out of the Israelites]~~ one man from each tribe, and said 5 to them, '~~[Cross]~~ over in front of the Ark of the LORD your God as far as the middle of the Jordan, and let each of you take ~~[a stone]~~ upon 6 ~~[it]~~ on his shoulder, one for each of the tribes of Israel. These stones are to stand as a memorial among you[~~[and]~~ in days to come, when your children ask you what these stones mean, you ~~[shall]~~ tell them 7 how the waters of the Jordan were cut off before the Ark of the Covenant of the LORD when it crossed the Jordan[~~[Thus these]~~ stones will always be a reminder to the Israelites.' The Israelites did as Joshua 8 had commanded: they ~~[lifted]~~ up

~~[f]~~ ~~of the LORD: prob. rdg., cp. verse 17; Heb. om[~~

fn: 3:16 Dead Sea : lit. Salt Sea.

221

A page of The New English Bible marked for revision

The revisers were charged to look out for and remove another kind of 'ism', the so-called 'briticism' – a word or phrase understood or used differently in Britain from other parts of the English-speaking world. When the NEB appeared a number of adverse comments about such words had been made, especially in the USA, and while they seldom led to actual misunderstanding, in some cases they caused stumbling by non-UK readers, or generated associations that were better avoided. The revisers often found that the briticisms complained of were not as well expressed in English as they might have been, and welcomed the opportunity to make a change. No form of English has an absolutely standardized vocabulary, and every country has its own regional variations. The NEB did not exclude regionalisms rigorously, except where they might have been unintelligible or ambiguous, and the presence of a number of Scots among the translators (as well as among the revisers later) provided some enrichment of the range of idiom. Some expressions claimed to be briticisms were found to be regional variations in common use in some parts of America; others were readily accepted in a biblical context. Nevertheless there were a number of changes that had to be made; for example, the domestic donkey – even Balaam's – may not be referred to as an 'ass', a plain indecency in the USA.

An important enlargement of the revisers' brief was to take account of the movement towards the use of gender-inclusive language in worship and scripture. From the early 1970s onwards, strong feelings about this issue were expressed in church circles throughout the English-speaking world, nowhere more fiercely than in the USA. As one American author writes, 'Once the issue has been raised, we become increasingly sensitized . . . We become more and more aware how often public speakers, ministers, writers use male words . . . One begins to lose the points of sermons while fuming over statements like "Christ died for all men" and

"God in Christ became man." The pain and anger become excruciating.'*

For the conscientious Bible translator this raises serious problems. The languages and cultures in which the ancient texts of the Bible were composed were male-oriented, the social order which formed their background male-dominated. To conceptualize in gender-inclusive terms was not an option for the biblical writer. Biblical translators down to the 1960s, when the NEB panels completed their work, felt no pressure to vary what were taken to be the gender terms used by the ancients.

The revisers, working under the direction of representatives of Churches which themselves were still in the process of coming to terms with the gender issue, felt the tensions keenly. It might have been possible, by rule of thumb, to divide the words traditionally translated 'man' into gender-specific (*aner* in Greek and *ish* in Hebrew) and non-specific (*anthropos* in Greek and *adam* in Hebrew) and render them accordingly. But the ancients, who had not anticipated the concerns of the late twentieth century, did not always observe these distinctions strictly; to have used them as a systematic basis for translation would have resulted in anomalies, uncertainties, and even absurdities.

It was not only ancient languages which threw up difficulties. Modern English is itself quite inadequate to cope in a fluent and natural way with all that needs to be expressed in gender-inclusive terms. Over-use of the word 'person' is foreign to idiomatic English and deadly to literary style. More than minimal use of the unspecific pronoun 'one' reads like a crude caricature of upper-class speech. Sometimes, but not always, it is possible while remaining faithful to the sense to render in the inclusive plural a noun or pronoun which is singular and male in the original; adjectival nouns in English

* Nancy A. Hardesty, *Inclusive Language in the Church* (Atlanta, 1987).

('the wicked' meaning wicked people, etc.) cannot normally be used in a singular sense.

Faithfulness to the original demanded that the masculine gender should be retained in references to God and the metaphorical use of terms like 'king' and 'son'. But where it was consistent with the context and the language of the ancient text, 'sons' became 'children' or 'descendants', and 'fathers' 'parents' or perhaps 'ancestors'. 'Brothers' was in many cases revised to 'brothers and sisters' or even 'friends'. In brief, the revisers' approach was to use a term which was inclusive or non-specific in gender wherever that sense was in their judgement consistent with the meaning of the original in its context, and acceptable in normal English style and usage.

Many of the criticisms of the NEB had to do with the 'high' level of the language. The gibe that the NEB was 'translated by dons for dons' (i.e. by scholars for scholars) was not altogether fair – it was a translation primarily for the reader with time to think about the meaning and to give the unexpected word a second glance, and not for the listener who must understand the passage as spoken or lose it for ever. Nevertheless there was much greater use of technical, literary, or 'dictionary' words than was either necessary or desirable. 'The effulgence of God's splendour' (NEB Hebrews 1:3) came to epitomize for the Joint Committee and the revisers the kind of phrase that might prove a stumbling block to a listener – though there were reservations that 'the radiance of God's glory' (REB) might not quite convey the intensity of image that was wanted. On the other hand, reducing the level of the vocabulary sometimes led to the sense of the original being conveyed in a more exact way, as when 'Let your magnanimity be manifest to all' (NEB Philippians 4:5) became 'Be known to everyone for your consideration of others.' The Joint Committee took great interest in the level of language used in the revision, and in one of several discussions of the subject, warned against the systematic rejection of polysyllables, reminding the Director and his team of the arresting effect of unusual words and the way they could help to give an appropriate flavour of, for example, solemnity to a particular passage.

Another 'donnish' feature of the NEB translation was the technical precision of some of its renderings, bewildering to the inexpert, but perhaps not always as perfectly understood by the translator as the confident use of a specialized term might indicate. The 'ruffed bustard' (? *Chlamydotis undulata*) of Zephaniah 2:14 (NEB) places a strain on the understanding of the unprepared listener, unlike the plain bustard of REB: yet uncertainty about the actual meaning of the Hebrew word is reflected in a whole menagerie of alternatives in other translations – from heron and screech-owl to hedgehog and porcupine.

At times, however, the right technical term must be used, and the revisers took care, for example, to adopt the currently preferred form of specialized expressions to do with the religious practices of the Jews. Thus the 'sin-offering' of NEB became 'purification-offering' in the passages of the Pentateuch where ritual observances are prescribed.

Footnotes are often regarded as a vice of scholars, but few serious translations of the Bible manage without notes of some kind. One of King James I's rules for the translators of the Authorized Version anticipated the need to exercise restraint:

> VI. No marginal notes at all to be affixed, but only for the explanation of the Greek or Hebrew words, which cannot without some circumlocutions so briefly and fitly be expressed in the text.

The notes in the NEB, particularly in the Old Testament, were on a generous scale, and a number of subsidiary editions printed only a reduced selection. The revision offered an opportunity to review the need for certain categories of note, and to reduce the total number accordingly. Many of the notes in the NEB Old Testament provided a translation of the Hebrew reading of passages where the translators had elected to rely on the Greek Septuagint text. As a matter of policy the revisers reviewed all these passages with great care, so that wherever possible the Hebrew reading might be adopted instead. In a great many cases they were successful in restoring the Hebrew, and the need for explanatory footnotes was accordingly reduced. Excessive noting of parallel passages was pruned, explanations of the significance of Hebrew proper names were dropped except where necessary for understanding the point of the passage, and other notes of only marginal interest or use to the general reader were omitted.

The revisers' policy of looking again at the Hebrew to make further efforts to work out the significance of difficult readings was also applied in cases where the NEB translators had adopted alternative meanings derived from related words in other Semitic languages. At the time when the NEB was being made there was a good deal of enthusiasm for this method of seeking solutions for a problematic reading. The technique meant – in extreme cases – that a key to the meaning of a word used in a biblical text originating more than 2000 years ago might be found in that of one based on the same three-letter root in the Arabic language of today. In many passages the application of this philological technique produced valuable insights into biblical vocabulary; in others it led too easily to idiosyncratic and questionable renderings. Critical reflection by the revisers upon the technique and the results it had produced in the NEB led to reversion to the traditional understanding of a word or passage in a number of cases. For example, at Joshua 15:18 and Judges 1:14 the NEB translators, attempting to avoid rewriting the text as many scholars have done, originally rendered the Hebrew verb *tsanach* as 'she broke wind'. This meaning was suggested by the Akkadian verb *tsanachu*, 'to discharge (blood, excrement)', which is found associated with a different Akkadian root *saratu*, 'to break wind'. Further reflection and research persuaded the revisers to revert to the more traditional rendering 'she dismounted'.

It is sometimes difficult to be sure what the NEB's original critics meant by donnishness, but there are two other particular features of the writing which may provide supporting evidence for the charge. The first is what might be called self-conscious idiomatic writing, which often reads like the old-fashioned kind of school crib: a phrase is used which is recognizably idiomatic English when viewed in isolation, but feels wrong in tone or weight when read in context. At 2 Corinthians 8:10, for example, where Paul is about to urge his readers to continue their financial contributions to other churches, the NEB has: 'Here is my considered opinion on the matter. What I ask you to do is in you own interests.' The English idiom cannot be faulted; but Paul, skilled persuader that he evidently was, would hardly have used such a tone of almost bullying portentousness. The REB's 'Here is my advice, and I have your interests at heart' captures the lighter touch of friendly persuasion without any sacrifice of idiomatic fluency. In the NEB at 2 Corinthians 7:2, 'Do make a place for us in your hearts!' says Paul, the idiomatic compound verb suggesting the effusiveness of a society hostess; the REB restores it to the level and tone of Paul's discourse simply by dropping 'Do'.

Another occasional feature which the NEB's readers may have found donnish is convoluted or inverted phrasing, though this is of course by no means confined to or even characteristic of academic writing. Part of the difficulty of the NEB in this respect may have been due to insufficient attention to punctuation. There seems to have been something short of full understanding between the NEB translators and the joint publishers: normally the translators left decisions about punctuation to the copy editors and proofreaders; on the other hand, the editorial staff responsible for processing the scripts had been trained to treat with the greatest respect every detail of any copy as sensitive as a Bible text, and would not normally presume to make any changes to punctuation unless an obvious error cried out for correction. They were more than usually diffident while working on the NEB, because they knew the two publishers each had their own, in some respects substantially different, house rules.

In the course of revision it was possible to make a much more systematic approach to the problems of punctuation. Questions were raised throughout the successive updating of interim revised scripts, and by the time the text came into the hands of the copy editor a reasonably comprehensive set of guidelines for standard practice had been prepared and adopted after consultation with the Director of Revision.

Clear and logically sequenced phrase construction, and helpful, consistent, but not too lavish punctuation, were seen to be of crucial importance when stress was laid on the REB as a version for reading aloud in church. The mind of the listener, unlike the eye of the reader, cannot go back over an earlier phrase to reassess how it is related to what follows. In every sentence, each phrase must contain a logical joint that links it to the next, as in the articulation of the limbs of the body. If the knuckle-bone is connected to the shoulder-bone we shall never hear the word of the Lord. In the NEB the phrase order of the Hebrew was often retained, especially when it was also preserved in the AV, even though a modest rearrangement would have sounded more natural to modern ears. A very simple example occurs at 2 Chronicles 4:17, where a location is given for Solomon's metalworking plant. The NEB reads: 'In the Plain of the Jordan the king cast them, in the foundry between Succoth and Zeredah', but the REB rearranges the verse to 'The king cast them in the foundry between Succoth and Zeredah in the plain of Jordan.'

Despite the strong preference for the use of exclusively

short sentences in some versions of the Bible aimed (perhaps over-optimistically) at a universal readership, the revisers, like the original translators of the NEB, saw no merit in breaking up the entire text into a series of staccato main clauses. Continuity and a logical flow from one event of a narrative to the next, or from one phase of an argument to its successor, could best be preserved by allowing groupings of related events or ideas to suggest where breaks should occur. The ability to vary the length of sentences is an indispensable tool with which to create light and shade, appropriate variations of pace, and dramatic pointing in any piece of writing. The lack of any but the most rudimentary punctuation in the ancient texts, and the sometimes arbitrary or even mistaken articulation in traditional English versions such as the AV, encouraged the NEB translators to make a fresh assessment of the sentence composition in the light of their reading of the text, and the revisers adopted the same approach, sometimes reverting to a more traditional presentation (as in Genesis 1:1–2) and sometimes introducing new changes when they seemed to shed greater light on the passage concerned.

Many biblical passages are used in sung liturgy as well as in spoken worship. The best conditions for the effective musical setting of words are not necessarily identical with what is ideal for the spoken word, but the revisers made no attempt to provide specifically singable texts in the Psalms, or elsewhere. However, the interests of singing and speaking often coincide, noticeably in the need for strong endings to musical phrases and spoken sentences. The second section of the 'Benedictus' (Luke 1:72) in the NEB ends with the almost parenthetic words 'calling to mind his solemn covenant'. When read, they may be mumbled and thrown away; set to music, their location at the end of a section tends to give them a misplaced emphasis that belongs more properly to the main clause. The REB avoids both dangers by reversing the order of the last two clauses:

> that, calling to mind his solemn covenant,
> he would deal mercifully with our fathers.

The shifting of the main clause to the end gives shape and force to the words, whether spoken or sung.

In rendering both Greek and Hebrew into English, the Bible translator is constantly faced with the difficulty that both these ancient languages use connective words (conjunctions such as 'and' and 'for') much more frequently than English. Their role is often little more than structural, to indicate that the words they introduce are a continuation of the preceding discourse. In modern English usage, on the other hand, such words are more usually expected to have actual meaning, to provide a logical, semantic link between one sentence and another. But the AV and more modern versions derived from it tend to use a connective in English wherever one occurs in the original, and this is one of those features which make traditional renderings of scripture so stylistically distinctive.

To a large extent the NEB translators followed the patterns set by their forebears. Typical of numberless examples might be the opening of a completely new section of the Letter to the Romans at 1:18 with the conjunction 'For', reflecting *gar* in the Greek, or the inappropriate 'And' at the beginning of 1 Kings 10:26. Both are avoided in the REB. On the other hand, when a genuine logical connective was present in the original, the revisers often found themselves able to take advantage of the fact that a stronger link between two statements may sometimes be established in English by juxtaposing them abruptly with no connective word.

In the course of revision it was possible to give additional help to the reader in understanding the structure of the writing. At a comparatively late stage of the work, the Joint Committee asked that thought should be given to the subheadings, not in the ancient sources, which had been introduced into the NEB to break up the text into extended sections for continuous reading, and to provide the traditional descriptive page headings to which Bible readers were accustomed. In many ways these had proved unsatisfactory. In order to avoid interrupting too often a text prepared essentially for continuous reading, the NEB editors had been very sparing in the provision of such headings. So much varied matter had to be covered by the same heading that they often became generalized to the point of meaninglessness. Either that, or headings appeared over passages of text to which they bore no discernible reference.

The potential use of subheadings to introduce, or give a context to, readings in church services led at first to the preparation of a very dense subheading structure for the revision. However, this approach came to be seen as unwise, partly in view of the danger that such headings might suggest 'interpretation' of the text, and partly bcause lections from the same general context might be prescribed for different liturgical purposes or seasons, beginning and ending at different points on different occasions. Moreover, some revisers felt that too heavy a density of headings tended actually to obscure the structure and message of the writing. A more elaborate heading scheme was therefore kept in reserve for the later school and study editions, where fragmentation of the text into 'gobbets' might be more useful, and a pattern was adopted for the standard editions based on using the subheadings to mark broad structural divisions of the text or significant changes of direction in the narrative or argument.

The adoption in the REB of the Hebrew headings to the Psalms, which had been omitted in the NEB, was a move by the revisers back towards a more traditional presentation. These headings, which are found in ancient sources, but are not thought by scholars to belong to the original text, are translated literally in so far as some otherwise unknown words permit. The word *Selah* (omitted in the NEB), whose exact meaning is likewise unknown but which is probably some kind of rubric or musical direction, is also reproduced in the REB where it occurs at the end of individual verses of certain Psalms.

A special feature of some editions of the NEB was the attempt to demonstrate the structure of Hebrew poetry by indenting lines differently in order to indicate the differing number of accents in the Hebrew line. This was in some sense in conflict with the general principle of the translation that it should reflect current English usage. Such a feature is not needed in English poetry and is certainly not a convention that is useful or meaningful to the average reader. It is in any case impracticable to follow it in double-column typesetting, and it was abandoned in the REB. In general, the poetry in the REB is structured in shorter lines than that in the NEB; where the beginning of the line is indented it indicates a turnover, i.e. that it is a continuation of the line above, which is too long for the width of the column.

The changes made by the revisers of the NEB are illustrated in this chapter by a series of simple and often trivial instances. An idea of the great number of changes throughout the version, and the importance of very many of them, can only be gained by reading the whole of both texts side by side, though it is doubtful whether such an exercise would have more than curiosity value. That the work of the revisers has produced a Bible which will stand for many years as a convincingly contemporary text seems beyond question.

7. THE PRINTED BOOK

Consideration of the form in which The Revised English Bible was to be presented to the reader began several years before the revisers had completed their work. Everyone concerned with the preparation of the REB had preconceptions about how it would appear in print, and it was necessary to make sure that they could be translated into a specification for a real book. There was also possibly a need to reconcile conflicting preconceptions arising from the different viewpoints involved – the member of the Joint Committee who perhaps saw it with the eye of the clergy, the reviser with the eye of a teacher, the publisher with the eye of an editor, a manufacturer, a salesman, or a common reader.

The NEB had been designed as a text that would be used for comparative study or general reading. The original editions – the so-called standard and library editions – were not at any stage thought of as 'church' books; indeed, the brief to the designer of the elegant library edition specifically asked that it should be presented like a high-quality literary novel. The use of the typography of the standard edition in a photographically enlarged form for church use as a lectern Bible, in order to save the very high cost of typesetting again from scratch, produced a notably unsatisfactory result.

The REB, on the other hand, was treated from the beginning as a book that must lend itself to use by Christian worshippers, whether in church or for private devotion, while still being acceptable for study and general reading. This meant a quite different design approach from that adopted for the primary editions of the NEB. Two changed characteristics were seen at once to be essential: that the page should be arranged in two columns, and that the verse numbers should be located in their exact position in the text.

Double-column setting was chosen so that the eye can travel more easily back from the end of one short line to the beginning of the next; setting in longer lines needs much more inter-line space to avoid confusing the reader's eye, and is thus uneconomical. For church use the reader must be able to locate a citation or the beginning of a reading exactly; in the NEB, verse numbers were placed in the margin of the page, and it is often impossible to guess within ten words or more where a particular verse begins – although figures in the margin rather than the text avoid being an obstacle to continuous reading.

The need for a third kind of change soon became apparent. Although footnotes would be needed in the REB, those responsible for the revision were reluctant to thrust them at the reader, in the standard editions at least. There was a reaction against what might appear to the general reader as an academic type of presentation. Those who were responsible for briefing the designer felt that the presence of footnote markers as well as verse numbers in the body of the text would create a clutter that would interfere with readability. At the same time the reader needed to be made aware at once of anything that could help him to understand a difficulty or oddity that he might meet in reading the text. The solution proposed was to omit markers in the text, but to give in the footnotes the chapter and verse reference along with the 'keywords' of the passage concerned, highlighted in bold type for immediate identification.

The choice of a typeface for the REB was made under entirely different conditions from those applicable to the NEB. In the period between the production of the two versions a revolution in typesetting methods had come to pass. The NEB had been set in metal type for letterpress printing, a technique almost entirely superseded for conventional book printing by the time of the REB. No longer was it practicable to cast each word character by character in molten metal; instead the printing image was to be prepared on a piece of two-dimensional film using a computer to assist in the generation of blocks of text photographically. The film would be used as an intermediate to make an offset lithographic printing plate. The almost universal adoption of this method of composition gave rise to a new range of type designs with different characteristics from those which produced good, legible results by inking a raised image and pressing it down on a piece of paper. Letterpress typography had evolved in a period in which Bible production had been a proportionally much more important and influential category of printing than it is today, and a group of typeface designs had become established which were particularly appropriate for use in texts of the Bible because of their density, compactness, dignity, and legibility in relatively small sizes. Generally these faces did not perform so well when converted for origination through film for offset printing. New type designs suited to the medium were developed, but the long experience which had made the selection of typefaces for specialized use like a Bible a matter of instinct had to be acquired all over again.

The editorial, production, and design staff of the two University Presses started to consult about the specification early in 1982. First, ideas about the overall size and shape of the book and the type area of the individual page were aired, having regard to ease of handling and reading, the economics of accommodating the huge number of words, and so on. Recently published Bibles and comparable books were studied, their good points noted and their weaknesses avoided. A selection of specimen passages from the interim revised texts with varying characteristics and problems was made in order to provide a frame of reference for the discussion. Finally some dozens of possible typefaces were evaluated, and a short list of six was picked in which extended passages of the different kinds of text were set and printed, so that comparisons could be made by a number of people under conditions approximating to 'real life' use. In these printed specimens varying treatments of features like footnotes, verse numbers, and headings were also tried out.

The specimen settings were compared by a joint production and design committee of the Presses in the light of comments received. The typeface Photina was found to conform most closely to the criteria applied by everyone: the clarity and evenness of the characters in the desired size; its compactness and economy; the brightness and liveliness of the page in double-column setting; the good balance between roman and italic and between letters and numbers. The designer, Paul Luna of Oxford University Press, was asked to prepare a full typographical specification, but this remained subject to minor revision throughout the typesetting process as local problems arose which could not have been foreseen during the basic discussions of the design.

Alongside the revolution in typesetting technology described above, the period between the making of the NEB and the REB saw technological progress of another, related kind, which contributed to the ease with which the revisers were able to consider the progressive results of their work, especially in the later stages of the revision. By the end of the 1980s the use of word processors to edit and store text, in a form which can ultimately be used directly for typesetting, had become completely conventional. But early in 1984, when the interim revised text of the REB began to be established in this form, there was still some uncertainty about the reliability of processors and more particularly about the automatic conversion of their product into printable typesetting. Every publisher, it seemed, could tell hair-raising stories about word-processor disks which refused expensively to be 'milked' and conversion programs which yielded only gobbledegook. The commitment of anything as vast as a complete text of the Bible to such a system was still in some sense an act of faith. But the rapid updating and playing out of

Diane Quarrie who keyboarded the whole REB text

successive revisions on the word processor was in any case a major improvement on the earlier procedure of retyping the entire script of a book after each round of revision. It reduced the possibility of errors creeping in, and made word-for-word reading of the retyped script unnecessary (although of course any amended passages had to be checked).

The Presses decided to work with a straightforward and relatively unsophisticated system (AES Alphaplus 12) which had been in use in the Cambridge office for administrative purposes for some time. The process of keyboarding the entire text of the revision as it then stood, entrusted to one freelance operator Diane Quarrie, was spread over a number of months, both to avoid inputting texts which were in the middle of active revision, and to prevent operator fatigue. A simple scheme of setting rules made it possible to produce printouts which had no typographic coding which would obstruct reading and checking, but at the same time would enable the system which would eventually convert the word-processor disks for typesetting to recognize automatically the difference between text and footnotes or prose and poetry, and identify features such as new chapter numbers even when they occurred (as they do) in the middle of sentences. Diane Quarrie quickly developed, as well as an unerring skill in applying these rules, an uncanny instinct for spotting anomalies in the copy that had emerged from the revision committees – inadvertently omitted or misplaced words or verse numbers, or inappropriate punctuation – and frequently alerted the Director to a need for further attention.

Although much of the work of the revision teams had been completed by the time the books came to be keyboarded, the adjustment of the text was by no means over. It was at this stage that scripts began to be made available to the members of the Joint Committee of the Churches for critical comment and suggestions. These were sent to the offices of the Presses and accumulated on a further set of word-processor disks so that they could be presented for consideration by the Director and his colleagues. In many cases these comments were supplemented by points noted by the staff of the Presses in the course of processing or proofreading the scripts. The New Testament review (see page 41) and the reconstruction of the subheadings led in turn to amended scripts being generated by the word processor, each stage being subject to a proofreading which might raise further queries. Finally, when the Director was satisfied that every criticism or suggestion had been duly considered and appropriately acted upon, the script for each book was presented to the copy editor Susan Moore.

The role of the copy editor in a book as huge, diverse, and sensitive as the Bible is a vital one. Rational and consistent treatment of such elements as spelling, punctuation, hyphenation, capitalization, and so on, not only reinforces the authority and usability of the printed product; it may in many cases have a bearing on the meaning of the copy. Susan Moore, a classical specialist, had little direct experience of dealing with biblical copy when first drawn into the work on the REB early in 1983. At that stage her function was a consultative one, examining interim texts to pinpoint those features and problems of presentation about which decisions in principle would need to be taken, in order to save expensive and complex later adjustment in proof. Like keyboarding, copy editing is most consistently, and so efficiently, carried out by one individual. The long production cycle inevitable in the preparation of a new Bible version happily makes this possible, despite being an apparent bottleneck and source of delay.

The time devoted to examination of earlier versions of the copy in and after 1983 had not been wasted. By the time the final texts started to arrive late in 1987, there was in existence a 'style book' embodying decisions reached after discussion with the Director about the specific problems of the REB text, which could be used by the copy editor and proofreaders in conjunction with *Hart's Rules for Compositors and Readers,*

Susan Moore, the copy editor

the widely accepted authority on typographic style which bears the name of a former Printer to the University of Oxford.

The fact that this kind of more or less mechanical problem had largely been resolved in advance enabled the copy editor to devote more of her energies to looking out for the few remaining ambiguities or infelicities in the text. There were inevitably some of these, resulting perhaps from late changes whose relationship to the surrounding context had not been explored far enough, or imperfections left from the NEB out of respect for the older version which had become more noticeable after the revisers' attention. In work of this kind everyone has something extra to offer as a result of their own private preoccupations. Susan Moore's botanical interests led, for example, to a succession of doubts or objections on distinctive yellow sheets of paper with such headings as *Displicentia* ('Things unpleasing') being addressed to the Director on such subjects as the colour of coriander seeds (Exodus 16:31) and the identity of 'stinkwort' (Isaiah 7:19). She was also a discerning censor of gender language.

When the copy editor's queries had finally been resolved, her marked script formed the basis for final adjustment and verification of the word-processor disks, to which were now added certain typographic codes to provide for the automatic setting of small capitals, for example.

H. Charlesworth & Co. of Huddersfield converted the disk database, by means of specially written computer programs, into a form which could be used to drive filmsetting equipment. This was a complex procedure, involving not only the translation of the signals embodied in the keyboarding of the text on the word processor, but also the addition of the elaborate coding needed to reproduce the specific typefaces and sizes and detailed arrangement prescribed by the designer. Copy for the footnotes had to be extracted from the text and processed separately, so that they could be fitted into the right pages of the typeset book. Galley proofs of the text and footnotes were shown to the publishers to ensure there were no major faults in the system and that nothing significant had been left out. Then the text was broken up into pages, and page headings and numbers were added.

Copies of complete pages in made-up form were submitted as proofs to four expert freelance proofreaders engaged by the University Presses: Richard Jeffery, Denis Parker, Stanley Parker, and Stephen Ryan. Since the publishers had no prior experience of this precise configuration of keyboarding and typesetting procedures, they decided to submit the proofs to a pattern of checking almost as rigorous as would have been adopted with the superseded technology of the previous generation, in which a sensitive piece of setting such as a Bible would have been re-read as many as seven times in at least two successive stages of proof. As it was, the typematter was scanned no fewer than five times in total – in first page proof and then again, after the few errors marked had been corrected, in a revised proof. The procedure embraced reading both against copy and 'by eye', i.e. for sense without comparing it with typescript copy. At each stage the work of the proofreaders was collated by the copy editor, who referred difficulties when necessary to the Director of Revision.

When the final corrections had been made to the database, Charlesworth produced two sets of 'camera ready copy' from their Monotype Lasercomp typesetter, which were delivered to the Presses in the course of May 1989.

The first publication of an internationally used version of the Bible presents special problems to its publishers. The quantities needed are very large, on any scale; they should be available simultaneously in a great number of places; the logistical problems of moving great numbers of books over large distances need to be carefully provided for and kept to a minimum; where two versions (with and without Apocrypha) are on offer, the proportions needed of each may be difficult to gauge, as was seen in 1970; facilities must be

Binding at Bath Press

available for reprinting and rebinding at very short notice. At first the University Presses had planned to print and bind the REB, like the original editions of the NEB before it, in their own Printing Houses, which both had a centuries-old tradition of printing Bibles of superlative quality. But investigation of the size of the operation and the speed with which it would need to be completed, together with considerations of the economics of producing in plants ideally equipped for production on a rather different scale, led to a decision in 1987 to place the work with outside contractors. The closure of the main Oxford production facilities early in 1989 would in any case have made such a step inevitable, though that unwelcome event was in no way anticipated in 1987. Quotations were obtained from suppliers in the UK and the USA, the two areas where the largest sales were expected. Assessments of potential demand from the Presses' marketing departments indicated a volume of sales in each area well above the critical economic printing quantity, and it was decided in view of the logistical problems mentioned above to produce simultaneously on both sides of the Atlantic. This decision was amply justified in spring 1989 by a sudden increase in requirements for the USA due to the selection of The Revised English Bible by the prestigious Book of the Month Club.

The initial printing and binding contracts were accordingly awarded to The Bath Press in England and to R. R. Donnelley & Sons in the USA, both experienced Bible producers with which the publishers had each dealt successfully in the past. Paper for both printings of the new Bible, again taking advantage of international resources, was manufactured at the Braunstein company's mill at Thonon in France near the Swiss border. In addition to the hardback binding of the standard editions in England and the USA, an order for leather presentation bindings of the same edition was placed with the fine binders MacDermott & Chant Ltd of Enfield in the UK, for distribution throughout the world.

The first introduction of the REB to the book trade was through an exhibit at the Christian Booksellers' Convention in Blackpool in March 1989

It is not possible to regard the publication of The Revised English Bible in September 1989 as being as unique an event as that of 1961, or even as that of 1970. Amid the clamour for attention now made by many different versions of the scriptures it was necessary to establish in the mind of Bible readers generally the particular qualities they could expect to find in the REB.

To this end the publishers, strongly supported by the Joint Committee of the Churches, began a campaign designed to give information to a wide range of potential users, the first target being the Churches themselves. During the summer of 1988 a video film about the REB, introduced by the well-known television presenter Sheena McDonald, was made for the publishers by the Church of Scotland Film Unit. The Chairman, the Director, and a number of members of the Joint Committee all took part. From the following autumn this film was used as an introduction to a series of presentations made to groups of Church leaders, educationists, and liturgical specialists. In the spring of 1989, advertising of the new version began in a more public way, and the publishers followed up their presentations to the Churches by freely distributing to clergy a choice of six booklets containing readings from the REB, for Sunday worship from Easter to Pentecost 1989, according to the prescriptions of various official lectionaries. In addition they made extracts of the text available to clergy for study and evaluation in advance of publication. By the middle of the year bookshops throughout the British Isles were being invited to order copies of the REB in anticipation of an intensified campaign of advertising and promotion as publication approached. Parallel programmes were under way in the USA and Canada, Australia, and elsewhere.

8. THE REALIZATION
OF A VISION

In forty years the resources available to readers of the Bible in English have grown beyond the bounds of what might have been thought possible at the end of the second world war. Not only have new versions of the complete Bible – both direct translations and paraphrases – appeared on the scene; revisions of older translations have been published, and have then been revised in their turn. New separate renderings have been made of the Testaments, and of individual books or groups of books. An immense wealth of secondary literature has been written. In The Revised English Bible (as also in The New Jerusalem Bible of 1985) we have yet another category: a revision of what was itself until recently a completely new translation.

The period of all this activity has not only been a time of re-evaluation and change in the language and worship of the Christian Churches. There has also been a profound reappraisal of the way Christian doctrine is applied to every aspect of life – to social and political questions, to personal ethics, to ecological and environmental issues. In these circumstances the process of revising a translation of the Bible is not simply a matter of verbal modernization, of changing 'thou' to 'you'; the engagement of the scriptures to our whole way of life must come under scrutiny. It is because they have seen vital reference in the Bible to their own lives and times that scholars have been moved throughout the centuries to retranslate and revise in terms that better fit the language and culture of their own day. The books of the Bible are sacred, not because of their antiquity but because of their relevance. Revision does not mean reinterpretation in terms of topical events and ideas; it may mean adjusting words which are difficult to understand or apply at the present day, through being too exclusively linked to ancient culture, superseded practice, or out-of-date idiom.

The last four decades have also seen a revolution in the ecumenical thinking and working of the Churches. The new determination of Christian denominations to address tasks of common interest and general benefit together is nowhere better seen than in the making of the REB. What began in 1946 as an exercise by a kind of select Protestant Establishment became very quickly an enterprise in which as many Churches participated as had the size, organization, and will to do so, either in planning and supervision through the Joint Committee or in the work of the revision teams. Other Churches contributed through individual members who raised queries, comments, or criticisms on the published NEB text. The change in status of the Roman Catholic representatives from observers to full members of the Joint Committee was especially important, since it led to the involvement of two Catholic Old Testament scholars in the revision work, and of a New Testament scholar in the person of the late Bishop Christopher Butler as a Joint Committee critic of the revised text.

Working together has the effect of making the Churches more conscious of the things which they have in common, and concentrate on using versions of the Bible which are acceptable to all. In the past, a new version of the Bible might well be the banner of a breakaway faction in the Church; now it is more likely to be a rallying point for groups which would otherwise go separate ways. The readership of versions which emphasize a particular kind of theology or churchmanship may tend to decline as the breadth of ecumenical dialogue increases, and such translations are increasingly unlikely to be produced in the future.

The ecumenical dialogue itself tends to be productive of change in the Church; there is a genuine desire to reach

The device (above) designed by Reynolds Stone as an emblem for the
NEB, and the distinctive adaptation made for use with the REB

accommodations, where this can be done without compromising essential belief. Since differences in the past have often turned upon the literal understanding of scriptural passages, the possibility of reviewing the translation of scripture may be a potential instrument of reconciliation. For this reason, if for no other, the work of revising the Bible in English is likely to go on.

The work of scholarship, too, will go on. Even now there are fragments of a text of Tobit from the Dead Sea Scrolls which remain unpublished. New discoveries cannot be ruled out, and scholars will continue to reassess the evidence about the biblical texts they already possess, as knowledge of the archaeological and historical background continues to grow.

Most of all, our language is a living thing, growing and changing constantly. Now that the convention is established that the Bible must be available in the vocabulary and idiom of its current readers, further revision will be needed to ensure that it stays that way. The attitudes and preoccupations of society may be expected to develop and change, with repercussions on the language we use, just as the concern about attitudes to women in society is currently forcing change in our use of gender language.

In the light of all this, it is not possible to suggest that the appearance of the REB – or indeed of any other version – will put an end to the process of reappraising the translations of the Bible. However, a point of some significance in the history of Bible translation in English has been reached. The NEB was the first complete translation from the ancient tongues into contemporary language. As such, it played a pioneering role; there were no existing criteria against which it could be measured, and it had to be evaluated in practice, in the life of the Churches and of individual Christian people. From that evaluation much was learned about what still needed attention: the particular characteristics of a version for worship and for reading aloud; the unreformed biblicisms and briticisms; the level and technicality of style and vocabulary; the gender language. The results of this learning process have been built into the REB, and we may now be seeing for the first time the true realization of the vision of those who participated in the conference of 1946.

THE SPONSORING CHURCHES AND OTHER BODIES

The Joint Committee on The Revised English Bible comprises representatives of:

The Baptist Union of Great Britain
The Church of England
The Church of Scotland
The Council of Churches for Wales
The Irish Council of Churches
The London Yearly Meeting of the Religious Society of Friends
The Methodist Church of Great Britain
The Moravian Church in Great Britain and Ireland
The Roman Catholic Church in England and Wales
The Roman Catholic Church in Ireland
The Roman Catholic Church in Scotland
The Salvation Army
The United Reformed Church

The Bible Society
The National Bible Society of Scotland

OFFICERS OF THE JOINT COMMITTEE
1971–1989

Chairman   The Right Reverend and Right Honourable the
Lord Coggan

Vice-Chairman The Reverend Professor C. H. Dodd (to 1973;
after the death of Professor Dodd no
appointment was made to replace him, but The
Right Reverend Falkner Allison deputized on
occasion for the Chairman at meetings of the
Executive Committee)

Joint Directors The Reverend Professor C. H. Dodd (to 1973)
Professor Sir Godfrey Driver (to 1975)
The Reverend Professor W. D. McHardy

Secretary   The Reverend Professor J. K. S. Reid (to 1982;
after Professor Reid's retirement, Roger Coleman
acted as secretary)

(The Executive Committee comprises the Chairman, the Secretary,
the Directors, and the representatives of the University Presses.)

THE JOINT COMMITTEE
ON THE NEW ENGLISH BIBLE*

(former members shown in brackets)

(a) Substantive members

BAPTIST CHURCH	The Revd Dr D. S. Russell (The Revd Dr E. A. Payne)
CHURCH OF ENGLAND	The Right Revd Falkner Allison, The Revd Canon A. E. Harvey (The Ven. C. J. Stranks, The Revd Canon A. G. Widdess)
CHURCH OF SCOTLAND	The Very Revd Professor R. S. Barbour (The Revd Professor J. K. S. Reid)
CHURCHES IN WALES	The Most Revd G. O. Williams
CHURCHES IN IRELAND	The Revd Professor E. A. Russell (The Very Revd J. L. M. Haire)
SOCIETY OF FRIENDS	Rowena Loverance (Dr G. E. Boobyer)
METHODIST CHURCH	The Revd Professor K. Grayston (The Revd C. L. Mitton)
MORAVIAN CHURCH	The Right Revd G. Birtill
ROMAN CATHOLIC CHURCH IN ENGLAND AND WALES	The Revd Fr R. C. Fuller (The Right Revd B. C. Butler)
ROMAN CATHOLIC CHURCH IN IRELAND	The Revd Dr J. McPolin S J

* Known after December 1987 as 'The Joint Committee on The Revised English Bible'.

ROMAN CATHOLIC CHURCH IN SCOTLAND	The Revd Fr J. Foley
SALVATION ARMY	Major Ian Cooper
UNITED REFORMED CHURCH†	The Revd Dr W. Houston (The Revd Professor J. C. O'Neill)
THE BIBLE SOCIETY	The Revd Canon W. Andrew (The Revd Canon R. W. F. Wootton, The Revd N. B. Cryer)
THE NATIONAL BIBLE SOCIETY OF SCOTLAND	The Revd F. Macdonald (The Revd J. M. Alexander, The Revd A. B. Doig)
CAMBRIDGE UNIVERSITY PRESS	R. Coleman, D. B. Forbes, Dr R. J. Mynott (R. W. David, C. F. Eccleshare, P. E. V. Allin, M. H. Black)
OXFORD UNIVERSITY PRESS	Sir Roger Elliott, N. Lynn, A. Potter (Dr C. H. Roberts, Sir John Brown, P. J. Spicer, The Revd R. A. Denniston, J. K. Cordy, R. D. P. Charkin, R. N. H. Douglas)

(b) Alternate members

BAPTIST CHURCH	The Revd H. Mowvley (The Revd Dr G. R. Beasley-Murray)
CHURCH OF ENGLAND	The Revd Professor D. E. Nineham
CHURCH OF SCOTLAND	The Revd Professor N. W. Porteous
CHURCHES IN WALES	The Revd O. Evans (The Revd Dr W. T. Owen)

† Until the two Churches joined together to form the United Reformed Church in 1972 the Congregational Church was represented by The Revd J. Huxtable and the Presbyterian Church of England by The Revd Professor J. C. O'Neill.

CHURCHES IN IRELAND	The Revd Canon C. W. Quin
SOCIETY OF FRIENDS	(Miss E. I. Pinthus)
METHODIST CHURCH	The Revd S. C. Thexton (The Revd Professor K. Grayston)
MORAVIAN CHURCH	The Revd F. Linyard
ROMAN CATHOLIC CHURCH IN ENGLAND AND WALES	The Revd Fr J. Deehan (The Revd Fr R. C. Fuller)
ROMAN CATHOLIC CHURCH IN IRELAND	The Revd Professor J. Quinlan
ROMAN CATHOLIC CHURCH IN SCOTLAND	The Revd Fr T. Hanlon
SALVATION ARMY	Major Clifford Ashworth
UNITED REFORMED CHURCH*	The Revd R. K. Scopes
THE BIBLE SOCIETY	The Revd Dr P. Ellingworth (The Revd J. Weller)
THE NATIONAL BIBLE SOCIETY OF SCOTLAND	The Revd Professor R. S. Barbour (The Revd Professor W. Barclay)

* Before the formation of the United Reformed Church in 1972, the alternate representatives of the Congregational Church and the Presbyterian Church of England were, respectively, The Revd J. E. Newport and The Revd Professor J. Y. Campbell.

APPENDIX IV
THE REVISERS
AND LITERARY ADVISERS

REVISERS

The Revd Professor G. W. Anderson, The Very Revd Professor R. S. Barbour, The Revd Fr I. P. M. Brayley, S J, Dr S. P. Brock, The Revd Professor G. B. Caird, The Revd Dr P. Ellingworth, Dr R. P. Gordon, Professor M. D. Hooker, The Revd A. A. Macintosh, The Revd Professor W. McKane, The Revd Professor I. H. Marshall, The Revd Dr R. A. Mason, The Revd Dr I. Moir, The Revd Fr R. Murray, S J, The Revd Professor E. W. Nicholson, Dr C. H. Roberts, Dr R. B. Salters, Dr P. C. H. Wernberg-Møller, The Revd Professor M. F. Wiles

LITERARY ADVISERS

M. H. Black, Mrs M. Caird, J. K. Cordy, Baroness de Ward, The Revd Dr I. Gray, Dr P. Larkin, Miss Doris Martin, Dr C. H. Roberts, Sir Richard Southern, P. J. Spicer, Dr J. I. M. Stewart, Mary (Lady) Stewart.

'MAC': A PERSONAL NOTE

Cullen, with its Auld Kirk and big house, ancestral home of the earls of Seafield, has been a Scottish royal burgh for seven centuries. The town has grown inland, from the little harbour and Seatown of jumbled former homes of fisherfolk, uphill on either side of a broad and dignified thoroughfare. At the top of the hill the town comes abruptly to an end. From this vantage point the eye may take in a northern seascape sweeping from the Moray Firth backed by the hills of Cromarty in the west to the bleak, open waters towards Norway in the east. By day the light is bright and clear; at night there are the stars and the distant scintillations of oilrigs and the fishing vessels out of Buckie, maybe, or Fraserburgh. The weather is always good when I visit Cullen.

Here at the top of the hill is the home of one of Cullen's most distinguished sons, William Duff McHardy. Made a Burgess in 1975, he cherishes this honour as deeply as any of the laurels of a notable academic career in other parts of the island, for Cullen is where his roots are, and they are struck deep. Close by is the little town of Fordyce, whose Academy provided the foundation of the learning which took him to the universities of Aberdeen, Edinburgh, London (as Samuel Davidson Professor of Old Testament Studies), and Oxford (eventually as Regius Professor of Hebrew and Student of Christ Church), to name but a few of the institutions that would claim him as theirs.

But I must write of him as I know him, as the leader of a major enterprise in biblical translation. And as a friend.

I first met Mac in 1975, and I was frankly a little apprehensive. Regius Professors (of Hebrew, no less!) are not the kind of people with whom one rubs shoulders in the grocer's, and somehow the idea of his confinement to a wheelchair (for Mac has been disabled since very early childhood by poliomyelitis) made him all the more formidable a prospect. My instinct was wrong about the Regius chair, for he exercises his scholarship gently and discreetly as well as firmly. But the wheelchair is a different matter altogether, for it confers peremptory authority, as I am reminded every time I find myself acting as an auxiliary propellant. As each problem arises – an unexpected stairway, a narrow door, a rough terrain – it is instantly sized up and resolved in a lucid string of easily executed instructions: 'Approach this one backwards; tip the chair slightly; left wheel first, then right.' So it seems to be with the problems of translation: the intellect switches on, analyses, and programmes the steps to be taken to reach an unerringly foolproof solution.

There is always humour about: the piece of wood which forms an indispensable device for getting out of the chair and into a car is inevitably known as Max Planck. 'You're cheating!' shouts Mac to a paralysed lady gliding by in an electrically powered chair. 'No; I am,' responds her unencumbered companion, with an apologetic glance in my direction.

In the early days of our acquaintance, Mac and I had relatively little to do together, for this was before there were interim texts to be processed by the Presses, and the publishers' editorial involvement was over matters of general style and punctuation, and the answering of criticisms of, and questions about, the NEB text raised by outsiders. Most of these were handled by the Cambridge liturgical editor, Derek Bowen, another remarkable character, a man to whom almost total deafness resulting from war injury had given immense power of concentration, no matter how infinitesimal the detail under study. Mac had the greatest respect for Derek's special faculties and for his comprehensive knowledge of scripture; he had less difficulty in communicating with him than many of us, and much missed him after his early death in 1981. By this time Mac had been using Derek as a guinea pig to read and comment on the results of his work with the revisers from the point of view of a layman, the imaginary man-in-the-pew whom he set before the revisers as the typical reader of the results of their work. In actual fact Derek was probably too highly qualified for the task, and I was able to take it over with more assurance than I could bring to other aspects of the work that he did for the REB and for the Press. For me, sadness at losing as valuable and erudite a colleague as Derek was mitigated by the excitement of getting more involved with the work on the revision and of collaborating more actively with Mac.

It is almost as interesting to watch collaboration with Mac taking place as it is to participate in it. As chairman of a revision panel he would maintain a low profile, allowing the specialists to tackle the problems in their own way, intervening only to recall attention to the main point, or to suggest a way out of an impasse, yet all the time concentratedly alert, watching for aspects that had been overlooked, ambiguities that had remained undetected. And before the session's work was written up as a fair copy of the text, one could be sure that he had been over it once again, tightening up any looseness of structure or punctuation, noting any parallel passage for later comparison, checking decisions against those already made, and so on.

He would behave similarly when copy editor and editor raised problems; listening to the considerations with great concentration and judicial detachment, he would hear them out and then pronounce judgement. Yet he was always, with great good humour and patience, ready to hear his own judgement questioned, and to seek further advice about anything which gave rise to uneasiness among his collaborators. An expert in many fields himself, he unfailingly gives just weight to the expertise of others. On minor issues he would sometimes dig in his heels, over the retention of a favourite cliché or a noticeably Scottish turn of phrase; yet, mysteriously, almost nothing to which strong exception had been taken ever appeared in the final text.

The fund of energy is, it seems, inexhaustible. But I think I now know one at least of the circumstances that make this possible: the family. Mac's wife Vera was a constant source of support in the days when I first knew him in Oxford. All too soon after they had moved back to Scotland, she was taken ill and died in 1984. One of those people whom one instinctively describes as 'a lovely lady', she was a Quaker, with all the gentleness and dedication and firmness that customarily suggests. Their daughter Alison, a historian then lecturing at the University of Aberdeen, was never far away, and on the spot in Cullen itself Mac finds himself at the mercy (as he would say) of his three lively, busy, and charming sisters. Together with Mrs Roberts, who orders his house and garden with enviable perfection, they form a magic circle of continuing mutual support.

The environment, too, is a source of strength. To drive with Mac around his native countryside is a delight and an education. Perhaps because of his long residence elsewhere, Scotland and things Scottish all have a special meaning for him, which he gladly communicates to the admiring foreigner.

But this is all part of a great zest for life which derives, I suspect from a deep spiritual awareness and vitality. I write 'suspect' because Mac is inclined to be reticent in common conversation about spiritual matters. A minister of the Church of Scotland for most of his adult life, he is said to be a very good preacher, and I find it odd that I have never yet heard him preach in public. He certainly never preaches in private. He belongs to that stream of the Church of Scotland tradition whose underlying high principles provide the basis for a humane liberality of outlook. But perhaps I am wrong to look for formal preaching to someone who has devoted the greater part of his life and work to making the word of God more accessible and meaningful. Somewhere, there must be a sermon in that.

R. C.

INDEX